THE SAINTS
IN MY LIFE

THE SAINTS IN MY LIFE

My Favorite Spiritual Companions

Fr. Benedict J. Groeschel, CFR

Our Sunday Visitor Publishing Division
Our Sunday Visitor, Inc.
Huntington, IN 46750

Dedicated to all the religious sisters who taught us to love the saints.

Our Sunday Visitor Publishing Division
Our Sunday Visitor, Inc.
200 Noll Plaza
Huntington, IN 46750

bookpermissions@osv.com
1-800-348-2440

ISBN: 978-1-59276-081-7 (Inventory No. T1184)
LCCN: 2011937806

Cover design by Lindsey Riesen
Cover art: OSV Archive photo
Interior design by Sherri L. Hoffman

PRINTED IN THE UNITED STATES OF AMERICA

TABLE OF CONTENTS

Introduction

KNOWING AND LOVING THE SAINTS, studying their lives and words has been an important part of my more than seventy years on earth. In fact, I would say that devotion to the saints has played a role in almost every aspect of my life. The saints gave me wonderful models to follow when I was a young man hoping to enter religious life and eventually to be ordained to the priesthood. Whenever I arrived at a crossroad in my life, I could always find a saint who had been there before me, someone whose example I could follow, who could serve as a guide. The lives of the saints have given me courage when I needed it; the writings of the saints have given me insights that I never could have attained on my own; the friendship of the saints has given me hope and a kind of support that I could have found in no other way. Without devotion to the saints my life would have been immeasurably impoverished. It would have been like a life without friends, without mentors, without guides. I owe the saints quite a debt of gratitude.

As I look back on my life I can't remember a time when the saints were not there. Certainly I first heard of them from my parents, who showed me beautiful holy cards on which were pictured many of the most famous saints: Saint Joseph, Saint Francis, and most frequently, the Blessed Mother. As a small child, I was intrigued by these pictures, attracted by the mysterious glow that seemed to emanate from these people who were called saints and who lived so long ago. By the time I started Catholic school I already knew a little about the saints, and I was soon to learn a good deal more. The sisters taught us to love the saints and to read about them. It was then that I learned that some saints had exciting lives, that some—like Joan of Arc—had even led armies. The saints were a vital part of Catholic life and an especially vital part of a Catholic child's life at that time. Saints became our heroes; saints were the ones we wanted to imitate; they became our models—and that is exactly what they should have been.

When I was ordained to the priesthood back in 1959, the beautiful Litany of the Saints was chanted, as it is at every ordination. I remember the slow and majestic rhythms of the Gregorian chant as one saint after another was invoked. This litany overflows with the names of saints, with the names of those who have prepared the way for us and given everything to God and the Church. It seemed to me at the time as if this catalog of holy names could have gone on forever, and so it could have. I heard the names of apostles, evangelists, martyrs, confessors, priests, hermits, virgins, widows. Every category was filled with the names of saints, and the prayers of each saint were implored for those to be ordained. "*Ora pro nobis*," we chanted over and over again, asking each saint individually to "pray for us." As we chanted the Litany of the Saints, we knew that as priests we would never be alone, that we had the support of countless saints in heaven.

Do we realize how very Catholic such a thought really is? Do we understand the great gift we are given in the saints? As Catholics we know that we are never truly alone in our journey to God. We are, the Letter to the Hebrews tells us, surrounded by a great cloud of witnesses (see Heb 12:1). That's what the saints really are for Catholics, Orthodox Christians, and even some Anglicans. They are a cloud of witnesses who help us and support us on our journey to Christ. This poetic term "a cloud of witnesses" is something on which we might meditate as we begin our contemplation of the saints. We could also use some other evocative and poetic terms that the Church has long employed when speaking of saints and their relationship to us on earth. One such term would be the Mystical Body of Christ and another would be the Communion of Saints. Although these terms are not identical they refer in a general way to the same wonderful reality: as we make our difficult journey to God we are linked tightly and lovingly to countless others who are making or have made the same journey. We are linked through Christ Himself. We must never forget that the Church is more than what we see here, more than its buildings, its clergy, and its faithful. The Church is the Mystical Body of Christ and includes all the saints in heaven and all the holy souls in purgatory. We are one body, bound together by the love of Christ.

Through Christ we are so close to the saints in heaven that we have been given the great gift of prayer to them and the equally great gift of being able to receive the benefit of their prayer for us. A Catholic knows that saints are more than just good examples taken from history. They are living friends who are concerned about us, friends with whom we can form relationships, friends we will meet in eternal life, friends who yearn to help us. In much of Protestantism this is denied. For the Protestant each one of us is alone before God. For the Catholic and Orthodox Christian, however, we are never alone, for the love of Christ provides us with the Communion of Saints, with a "cloud of witnesses."

In the decline of Catholicism and of religion in general during the present period, the devotion to the saints has diminished along with many other things, including devotion to the Eucharist and to the other sacraments. Many Catholics do not know the saints at all, and this is a great tragedy, a huge loss. The Church has always canonized saints, at least in part, to give us examples, to show us what the Christian life should be. If we do not know anything about the many holy lives that have preceded us since the time of Christ, how can we really know what it is to be a Christian, to be a real Catholic? Saints show us the heights to which we can soar if we are truly united to Christ; they show us what holiness is in this earthly life and what it is possible for us to attain.

So I thought it was time to write a little book about saints. And this is a *little* book. It makes no effort to cover all the great multitude of saints who have been canonized. Neither does it make an effort to look at saints from every period of Church history or from every area of the world. This is a very personal book. It is not a Litany of the Saints. It is simply a part of *my personal* litany of the saints. Included in it are only a handful of my special friends. Some of them are saints to whom I've been devoted since I was a child; some are saints I've come to know in recent years. They are all, however, saints who have made an impact on my life. You probably know many of these saints, but there may be a few whose names you've never even heard before. If so, I hope you will use this book to make some new friends in heaven.

There is another way in which this book is very personal to me. Although I've included a brief biography of each of the saints about whom I have written, I freely admit that these biographies are seen through the prism of my personal devotion, my personal relationship to these saints. Perhaps someone else might emphasize different things in the lives of the same saints. That is one of the wonderful things about the saints: their lives are so full, so whole, so multi-dimensional, so brimming with meaning for us, that very different people can consider very different aspects of the lives of the same saints to be important.

I should also tell you that I very purposely did not write about the most important saints in my life: Saint Paul, Saint Peter, Saint Joseph, and (of course) the Blessed Mother. These are saints to whom I felt I could not do justice in a book such as this. In fact, I don't think I could do them justice under any circumstance. Each one deserves a separate volume, and even that would be painfully inadequate. I do, however, urge you to learn as much as you can about these great, great saints, for they should be the saints most beloved by every Catholic. We can lose ourselves in meditating on their lives. In these few great saints we can find an inexhaustible source of material for prayer and devotion, a constant source of growth and renewal in our spiritual lives.

I'm hoping that the reader of this book will be deeply affected by at least some of the saints about whom I've written. My goal is that you will find some element in the life of Saint Thérèse or Saint Maximilian Kolbe or Saint Clare that strikes a chord in you—as something about their lives strikes a chord in me. I'm hoping that you will begin to see what a saint is and how important to the life of every Catholic saints must be. I'm hoping that when you have finished this little book your appetite for saints will not be satiated but only whetted. I want you to read biographies of saints, to pray to saints every day. I'm hoping that every time you look at a Catholic calendar from now on you will be intrigued by the names of unknown saints, that you will try to find out about at least some of them. It's not impossible that you will find a special friend in heaven this way, one who will be important to you for the rest of your life.

Unexpected saints often become our closest friends, so don't look at saints with any preconceived notions, for they're often surprising. You may not think, for example, that a cloistered nun like Saint Teresa of Avila has anything to say to you. Well, think again. She is a saint with a dynamism that is almost unbelievable, and she has spoken deeply to the lives of countless people who never walked behind a cloister wall.

So let me begin my little litany of the saints; let me introduce you to a few of my best friends in heaven. We will start with a saint who, as a child, may have been held in the arms of Christ and we will end with a saint who, in his earthly life, actually sent me a card.

A SMALL NOTE

I'm sure there are going to be devout people who will be somewhat disappointed with this book because their favorite saint is not mentioned in it. Well, as I said, I'm just writing about a handful of the saints that *I* have especially loved. I have a suggestion for you: write about your favorite saint. Perhaps such an article might be published in a parish bulletin or even in a small local Catholic newspaper or magazine. You never know where such things may lead.

Saint Ignatius of Antioch

Just who is Saint Ignatius of Antioch? I suspect that many of my readers are asking this very question. Perhaps some have mistaken him for that more familiar Ignatius: Saint Ignatius Loyola, founder of the Jesuits. The names of many of the saints I will be discussing in this book are well known to most Catholics. A saint like Ignatius of Antioch, however, is different and perhaps a bit mysterious. We may not be sure of the time in which he lived—or even where he lived. I have a strong feeling that most people can't even locate Antioch on a map. It is, in fact, in present-day Syria and was one of the most important centers of the early Christian Church.

So let's begin at the beginning. Saint Ignatius of Antioch stands prominently among that group that we very reverently call the Fathers of the Church. He is one of the many theologians, teachers, priests, and bishops who were the great shepherds of the early Church as well as the guardians of her doctrine. The Fathers of the Church succeeded the apostles, and it was the Fathers who articulated and interpreted the very nature of Christianity to the world for the first few centuries after Christ. They did this not only through their own writings but through the decisions of the first seven councils of the Church.[1] After Holy Scripture, their work forms the bedrock and wellspring of Christian doctrine, and it always will. Their writings, which are often of vast theological depth, still inspire the Church today and guide her decisions. After the apostles and, of course, Christ Himself, the Fathers of the Church form the theological foundation upon which the edifice of the Church stands.

A Saint Who Knew No Fear

Ignatius of Antioch is one of the earliest of the Fathers of the Church. Along with Clement of Rome, Polycarp of Smyrna, and a few others, Ignatius was among the immediate successors of the Apostles. This group is often referred to as the Apostolic Fathers for just this reason: they were the ones closest to the source. They learned from the men chosen by Christ Himself. Ignatius of Antioch is so close to the time of Christ that he is generally thought to be a student of Saint John the Apostle. There is a longstanding tradition that Ignatius received his episcopal ordination as the third bishop of Antioch from Saint Peter himself. This would make good sense, as Peter was the first Bishop of Antioch. (Saint Evodius, of whom we know little, occupied the see between Peter and Ignatius.)

There is a wonderful legend about Ignatius concerning the child whom Christ picked up and held in his arms, as recorded in the Gospel of Mark. Saint Mark says: "And he took a child, and put him in the midst of them; and taking him in his arms, he said to them, 'Whoever receives one such child in my name receives me; and whoever receives me, receives not me but him who sent me'" (Mk 9:36-7). The early Church claimed that the boy held so tenderly by Jesus was none other than Ignatius. Is there any truth to this legend? Who knows? Whether this story is rooted in truth or not, however, it does show clearly how intimately tied the early Church believed Ignatius to be to the Apostles and to Christ. We also see the esteem in which the Church held this saint, for they believed him to be one of the few people who actually had received the great gift of physical contact with the Son of God during his earthly life. We see this esteem again when we look at the name the early Church often used for Ignatius, Theophorus, which in Greek means "God carrier." They believed that the child who was carried in the arms of Christ would be charged with carrying Christ to them. It's not an easy name or an easy concept to live up to, but I think Ignatius managed better than most.

It is difficult to sketch a real biography of one who lived so long ago and at a time when few records were made or kept. We must remember that during the time of Ignatius, the Church was a small, often despised, and regularly persecuted minority. Such circumstances do not lend themselves to good record keeping. We shall, therefore, look at some of the high points of Saint Ignatius's life and at his great accomplishments as found in the Church's Tradition and his own writing.

Ignatius was Bishop of Antioch at the time of the Domitian Persecutions, fierce attacks on Christians which took place roughly from 81 to 96. Tradition tells us that he was unstinting in his efforts to protect his flock, to inspire them and give them hope. During this difficult time, Bishop Ignatius was very visible. He did little to protect himself, choosing instead to protect those in his care. We see here a true shepherd of souls in action and an example that all bishops should look to today.

Although he survived the Domitian Persecution, Ignatius was not denied martyrdom. Early in the second century (perhaps around 107) the Emperor Trajan decreed that all people must worship the Roman gods throughout the empire. This was not a decree to be ignored, as refusal to follow it would result in death. Ignatius must have been well aware of this but resisted nonetheless—as was his duty as a Christian and a bishop.

Ignatius was soon arrested by the Imperial authorities, condemned to death, and transported to Rome to die in the arena. By dealing with a leader in this way, the Romans hoped to demoralize and terrify the followers, to scatter the sheep. Ignatius, however, was determined that this would not happen. His transport to

Rome as a prisoner in chains was carefully designed to make him look powerless, a pathetic object of ridicule. The Roman guards soon discovered, however, that things were not working according to plan. Far from cowering in fear or giving up, Ignatius is said to have taken every opportunity to encourage not only his Christian flock in Antioch, but Christians all along the way. He spoke to groups of Christians again and again at each town along the long road to his execution, exhorting them to persist in the faith despite the dangers and to love God and heaven more than life on earth. Journeys took a long time back then and were often characterized by many starts and stops. When Ignatius at last reached the west coast of Asia Minor (present-day Turkey), the prison guard stopped for a while before boarding a ship to Rome. During this hiatus, delegations from several churches in Asia Minor were able to visit the imprisoned bishop. They spoke and prayed with him and were even able to give him food and other items to make his journey less painful. They bade him farewell and emerged encouraged, their faith strengthened by his remarkable presence.

As if this were not enough for one on his way to execution, Ignatius used the time to write seven letters that have been preserved: five to congregations that had greeted him on his journey (Ephesians, Magnesians, Trallians, Philadelphians, and Smyrnaeans) and one to the congregation that greeted him at his destination (Romans). He wrote one more letter, this one to Saint Polycarp, who was then Bishop of Smyrna and, like himself, a disciple of Saint John the Apostle.

These letters are theologically dense and precise, and when they are read today it seems amazing that they could have been composed under such stressful conditions. They are powerful letters that are still regularly studied, so Ignatius still speaks to us from out of the distant past, still guiding us, as a bishop should. Clearly he was a pastor to the depths of his very soul, the kind of man every priest should want to be, a man who gives himself physically, spiritually, and intellectually to his flock, who gives himself fully, without fear of the consequences. He demonstrated at this time, just as he had demonstrated throughout his life, that he was totally committed to the service of God.

Saint Ignatius of Antioch met his death in 110. He was torn apart in the Roman arena by wild beasts for the amusement of a decadent Roman civilization. That Roman civilization is long since gone, but the influence of Ignatius of Antioch persists to this day and will continue for all time. In Saint Ignatius of Antioch we find a true Father of the Church, a priest, a bishop, a theologian, a martyr. He has been rightly and fittingly called an "athlete of God."

"We Have Not Only to Be Called Christians, but to Be Christians" [2]

I'm taking a chance by beginning this book with someone like Ignatius. He is certainly a great saint and one who has definitely meant a tremendous amount to me over many years. But let's face it: Ignatius of Antioch is not exactly cuddly. He may even be somewhat off-putting, and perhaps there is a danger that some of my readers may not want to progress further in this little book after contemplating the stern figure of Ignatius.

Well, I'm willing to take that chance because Ignatius of Antioch has a lot to teach us. We know only fragments—bits and pieces—of his life. Yet from the little that we do know we receive a powerful message. Perhaps we should even admit that it is a disturbing message. This very early saint brings home to us in no uncertain terms the fact that the Christian life requires an enormous amount from us. It requires nothing less than a transcendence of the self. Ignatius reminds us in a very uncompromising way that the Christian is not called to sacrifice occasionally, to give parts of himself when the circumstances call for it. This saint makes us acknowledge a fact we would prefer to forget or at least ignore: the Christian is called to give himself or herself totally to God, to count as nothing the things of this world. Ignatius's complete dedication as a priest and bishop, his fearlessness in the face of death, and his continued efforts to guide and teach his flock—even as he was going to his execution—all illustrate this. Perhaps Ignatius even makes this seem easy. It is not. But with the help of the Holy Spirit it is as possible for us as it was for Ignatius. We must say that such dedication does not happen overnight. Even Ignatius probably had to develop it over time. For most people progress in the Christian life is a slow and incremental process. The renunciation of self is the work of a lifetime, a work that engages us until we take our final breaths on earth. But it is work that we must do.

Ignatius's death was not one that anyone would choose for himself. Being torn apart by wild beasts for the entertainment of others is horrible even to contemplate. Yet Ignatius accepted as a blessing the knowledge that such a death was approaching. He was able to see beyond the pain and horror that awaited him with the eyes of profound faith. He was able to accept in the deep recesses of his heart and soul the fact that we live in a passing world, a dying world, but that through the death and resurrection of Christ we are given the grace to transcend the pain and death that we must face in our earthly lives. In our time and in our culture we may find this difficult to comprehend because we cling to life and the things of this world fearfully and very tenaciously.

I can only imagine what Ignatius of Antioch would have said about our contemporary culture and its attitude toward death. I am willing to bet that he would see it as no less shallow and pagan than the Roman world in which he lived, and I suspect he would find the Christianity of many of us rather shallow, as well. Our faith, compared with that of the early Christians, is weak, and this is shown most clearly in the way we understand death. The following words were written by a contemporary philosopher just a few years ago: "Christianity is about nothing other than getting ready to die. It is a rigorous training for death, a kind of death in life that places little value on longevity. Christianity in the hands of a Paul, an Augustine or a Luther is a way of becoming reconciled to the brevity of human life and giving up the desire for wealth, worldly goods and temporal power."[3] Do those strong words shock us a little? I am willing to bet that they do, but they would not have shocked Ignatius of Antioch. He would have understood them very well, although I suspect he would have considered them one-sided. For Ignatius, the renunciation of self and the things of this world have little meaning on their own. They are not merely "a way of becoming reconciled to the brevity of human life." They are a way of drawing ever closer to God. For Ignatius knew that what appears to be a great loss can, in fact, be the supreme blessing. He knew we can never really lose anything of value by putting ourselves, our works, our loves, our hopes, and our fears into the hands of God. He understood that it is only in this way that we can obtain anything of lasting value. Ignatius of Antioch knew, as did Saint Francis of Assisi many centuries later, that it is only "in dying that we are born to eternal life."

This early martyr is not very well known today, but he has been like an anchor to me over many, many years. Ignatius of Antioch is difficult. He calls Christians to a life without compromise. At first glance he may seem almost cold, as if he had no human emotions. But when you get to know him well, as I have, you find a different picture, one that is truly warm and inspirational. This stern saint is constantly pointing us in the direction of ultimate happiness. He reassures us that we really can see more clearly with the eyes of faith than the eyes of the world. He has taught me, and I hope he will teach you, to put all that we have, all that we are, into the hands of Christ, to abandon our fears—even our fear of death—and to trust in the love of God no matter what happens to us during our earthly lives.

─────

The following is taken from Saint Ignatius's "Letter to the Romans," which he composed shortly before his death. If we knew nothing of Ignatius before reading it, we would understand much of this great man by the time we were finished.

The delights of this world and all its kingdoms will not profit me. I would prefer to die in Jesus Christ than to rule over all the earth. I seek him who died for us. I desire him who rose for us. I am in the throes of being born again. Bear with me, my brothers; do not keep me from living; do not wish me to die. I desire to belong to God; do not give me over to the world, and do not seduce me with perishable things. Let me see the pure light; when I am there, I shall truly be a man at last. Let me imitate the sufferings of my God. If anyone has God in him, let him understand what I want and have sympathy for me, knowing what drives me on.

The prince of this world would snatch me away and destroy my desire to be with God. So let none of you who will be there give him help; side rather with me, that is, with God. Do not have Jesus Christ on your lips and the world in your hearts. Give envy no place among you. And if, when I get there I should beg for your intervention, pay no attention to me; no, believe instead what I am writing to you now. For I write to you while I yet live, but I long for death. My earthly desires have been crucified, and there no longer burns in me the love of perishable things, but a living water speaks within me saying: "Come to the Father."

I take no delight in corruptible food or in the pleasure of this life. I want the bread of God, which is the flesh of Jesus Christ, who was David's seed, and for drink I want his blood, the sign of his imperishable love.

I no longer wish to live, as men count life. And I shall have my way, if you wish it so. Wish it, then, so that you too may have God's favor. With these few words I beg you to believe me. Jesus Christ will make plain to you the truth of what I say; he is the true voice that speaks the Father's truth. Pray for me that I may reach my goal. I have written to you not prompted by merely human feelings and values, but by God's purpose for me. If I am to suffer, it will be because you loved me well; if I am rejected it will be because you hated me.[4]

SAINT AUGUSTINE

SAINTS SHOW US MANY THINGS. One of these is that there is hope for us all. We, who have been to Catholic schools, have a tendency to think of saints as having God uppermost in their thoughts at all times. Yet the early lives of some saints give us ample proof that this was not always so. It is no understatement to say that quite a few saints were far from perfect before they reached that mysterious moment when everything changed through the mystery of God's grace, when they were suddenly grasped by faith in a way that was both new and overpowering. Saint Paul on the road to Damascus is the prototype of this, but he was only the first of a long list that continues down through the centuries.

More than a few saints seemed utterly hopeless in the earlier parts of their lives, and we are about to encounter such a saint now. Saint Augustine is one of the great giants in the history of the Church. He is a theologian whose influence is impossible to overstate. He can legitimately be called the primary theologian of the Western Church. Yet Augustine got off to a bad start—to put it mildly. As a youth he was worldly and fell into just about every type of sin that young, worldly men are likely to fall into—and that's quite a few! As if that were not enough, he enthusiastically embraced the major heresy of his time. His early life would certainly not have led anyone to believe that holiness would be probable for him. Yet, his mother, Saint Monica (whom we shall consider in the next chapter), prayed fervently for years that her son would not be lost to sin. For a long time it seemed as if her prayers were in vain, but finally they were answered in a way that must have infinitely exceeded her fondest wish. In the story of Saint Monica's concern for Augustine's salvation I believe we can learn much about prayer, perseverance, and patience. We can learn to trust God to work things out in His own time and in His own way.

Many saints have meant a great deal to me, but if you know me, you know that few have had the effect that Saint Augustine has had. Aside from Saint Francis, Saint Augustine of Hippo has had more influence on me than any other saint, so I am very happy to offer you a look at the life of this great saint who began so unpromisingly.

The Restless Saint Who Found His Rest in God

Saint Augustine was born on November 13, 354, about a century and a half after the death of Saint Ignatius. Like Ignatius, Augustine is one of the Fathers of the Church, but he is much better known to us. His writings are voluminous. They are also very introspective and perceptive, and from them we learn the bulk of what we know about him. His autobiography, the *Confessions,* is one of the great books of Western literature, as well as one of the great books of the Church.

Augustine was born in Tagaste, in the Roman province of Carthage (present-day Algeria), to a family that, although upper class, was not wealthy. From the beginning he was subject to conflicting influences—pulled in opposite directions at once. His father, Patricius, was a pagan and not at all friendly to Christianity. His mother, Monica, however, was a devout Christian who yearned for her family to follow Christ. As a boy, Augustine was sent by his father to be schooled in Madaurus, a largely pagan town that was nearby. Yet his mother also made sure he received a Christian education and enrolled him among the catechumens in preparation for baptism.[1] These two influences would fight for dominance in Augustine's life for quite some time.

The pull between paganism and Christianity was not the only tension in Augustine's early life. The Roman world of his youth was extremely sensual and given to excess; and like many young men, Augustine easily fell prey to this. He was highly intelligent and at the age of seventeen was sent to the city of Carthage to study rhetoric. Yet at about the same time he entered into a relationship with an unnamed young woman and fathered an illegitimate son, whom he named Adeodatus.[2] He stayed with this woman for fifteen years without ever marrying her. In Carthage Augustine encountered Manichaeism, a form of Gnosticism that had won many converts from the Church and from the Roman pagan world. It was profoundly dualistic, positing a world of light and goodness pitted against a world of darkness and evil. Augustine was deeply attracted to the ideas of Manichaeism and soon fell under the spell of this heresy.

As I said earlier, Augustine got off to a bad start.

After completing his studies, he returned to Tagaste to teach and quickly developed a wide circle of followers who were attracted by his deep and undeniable intelligence. Monica, however, despairing of her son's new heresy, seemed to reach her limit. For a time she refused to let him into her home. It is said that she relented only when her bishop told her "the son of so many tears could not perish." Successful but restless, Augustine was soon on the move again. He had left the city of Carthage as a student; now he returned to it as a teacher, once again attracting large circles of students, just as he had done in Tagaste. During this period, however, Augustine began to look more closely at Manichaeism, perceiving its flaws and contradictions for the first time. He finally broke with it but only after nearly ten years in its thrall.

In 383 he decided to go to Rome. Monica, however, was desperate that her twenty-nine-year-old son should not leave.

Certainly encouraged by the fact that Augustine was no longer a formal heretic, she was probably afraid of the new ideas he would encounter in Europe. Augustine, however, still far from the saint he would become, was determined to go. Like a little boy running away from home, he left without telling his mother the date of his departure. He made his way to Rome, teaching there for a while, and then going to Milan, and—although he surely had no idea—to the Church he had avoided his entire life.

In Milan Augustine encountered Bishop Ambrose [3] and became fascinated both by the bishop's kindness and his preaching. Here, possibly for the first time, Augustine heard the truths of the Church expounded in a way that was both filled with love and utterly free of error. The two men became good friends. Yet even now, at the age of about thirty, he declined to enter the Church, for once again he found himself torn. He could not force himself to turn his back on the life of prestige and sensuality that he was leading.

But someone with a soul as great as Augustine's could not remain indecisive forever. Seeing men of lesser intelligence and fervor leaving lives of sensuality behind and being baptized, he was overcome with shame that he could not do the same. In the summer of 386 Augustine read about Saint Anthony, the desert saint, who was beset by many temptations, yet overcame them all. This made him acutely aware of his own failures. He wrestled with this for months, desiring to convert, yet feeling utterly unable to do so. Finally, he seemed to hear God saying to him: "Take and read." Augustine opened the Bible and read the words of Saint Paul: "But put on the Lord Jesus Christ, and make no provisions for the flesh, to gratify its desires" (Rom 13:14). This decided things for him, bringing all his mother's prayers and Ambrose's teachings to fruition together. In the presence of a very relieved Monica, Augustine and his son, Adeodatus, were baptized by Ambrose during the Easter vigil in 387.

After his baptism, his life seemed to be transformed. The problems that had plagued him earlier were overcome, and Augustine set about becoming the saint that he was meant to be. He returned to Africa,[4] where he sold nearly all of his personal possessions and gave the money to the poor. He converted his home into a kind of monastery for himself and a few others who were similarly devoted to the Church. Augustine was ordained to the priesthood and became a powerful preacher, often combating the very Manichaeism that he had once supported. In 395 he became Bishop of Hippo, a position he retained for the rest of his life.

This was a very difficult period in the history of the Roman Empire. Things were coming apart at the seams. Barbarian tribes were making greater and greater inroads into the once impregnable empire; and, as the political situation deteriorated, so did the religious one. Heresies and schisms abounded, deeply threatening the Church. Augustine powerfully resisted these. First he combated the Donatists, who asserted that it was the personal holiness of a priest or bishop that made his sacraments valid. Understanding only too well the weakness of human nature and seeing clearly that such a view would make almost all sacraments suspect, Augustine forcefully made the case that it was the ordination of the priest or bishop that gave validity to his sacraments regardless of personal purity. In the course of combating this heresy Augustine developed theories of the Church and of the sacraments that still stand today. He also developed his just-war theory, which has influenced the Church up to the present moment. This teaching of Saint Augustine actually prevented or even ended many wars throughout European history.

Augustine also confronted Pelagianism, a heresy that denied original sin and implied that man can reach salvation unaided by the grace of God. Obviously such a view contradicted the very life that Augustine had lived, the lives that he had seen others live around him. Introspective and given to brilliant self-analysis, he knew only too well the innate disorder in the human soul, for this is what had caused him to wrestle for so many years with his own sinful tendencies. How could there be any truth in the Pelagian opinion when every human life seems to contradict it? Augustine's thinking on original sin is deep and complex; it has shaped the Church's dogma for centuries. We will not go into that here, as that would take a large volume, but I suspect he would have approved of the words of the Protestant theologian Karl Barth, who wrote that original sin is "the doctrine which emerges from all honest study of history."[5]

Augustine was extraordinarily effective in his struggles with Pelagianism, and he was just as effective toward the end of his life when he combated another heresy called Arianism, which maintained that the Second Person of the Holy Trinity as well as the Third were somehow less than the First—obviously a reversion to polytheism. This was a great risk in the first few centuries after Christ. Large numbers of former pagans were converting to Christianity, and although their motives may have been sincere, they could not help but bring with them ideas from the religions in which they had been brought up. Gods of various ranks as well as demigods populated the mythologies of the ancient world, so it was almost unavoidable that some former pagans would think of Christ in this way. Again Augustine saw the problem and combated it with every bit of his great intellect and formidable faith. Arianism proved a powerful foe and endangered the Church for many years, returning again and again in different forms. Its final defeat, however, was due in no small part to Augustine's clear and potent arguments against it.

Augustine, the former heretic, struggled mightily with one heresy after another, always asserting and explaining the truths of the Church in ways that were not only forceful but so intellectually sound that they remain virtually unassailable. He laid down a beautiful and profound theological framework that still remains in place today. Augustine, the great soul, delved deeply into his own psyche and that of others, producing insights and understandings of the human spirit that have guided religious thinkers as diverse as Saint Bonaventure, Kierkegaard, and our present Holy Father, Benedict XVI.

Augustine departed this life on August 28, 430. More than a millennium and a half later his influence is everywhere. His philosophical and theological accomplishments and dedication to Christ have rarely been equaled and certainly never surpassed.

Not bad for a boy who started out so poorly.

THOUGHTS ABOUT AN OLD FRIEND

How can I write about Saint Augustine in only a few pages? For well over sixty years he has been my constant companion. He is the one to whom I turn when I am perplexed. His wisdom and deep theological, philosophical, and psychological insight have been an unending source of encouragement and excitement to me for such a long time that I cannot imagine what my life or my priesthood would have been without him. Whatever I say in this little book will simply scratch the surface, and I urge all my readers to learn more about Saint Augustine, to delve into this saint's magnificent writings. I can guarantee that you will find such an effort immensely rewarding.

I remember the day I met Saint Augustine. I was fourteen years old, and I read the opening pages of the *Confessions*, which contain one of his most famous lines: "O God, Thou hast made us for Thyself, and our hearts are restless until they find their rest in Thee." I was stopped dead in my tracks. I had never read words like these before. They seemed both intensely beautiful and absolutely true, and I kept repeating them over and over again in my mind. As a very young person who was contemplating the religious life, I was only then becoming aware of the restlessness of life of which Saint Augustine speaks, the search that attends every human existence. Perhaps I was beginning to sense the uncertainty and ambiguity that face us all when the security of childhood ends and the rest of life, with its endless choices, opens before us. In these words of Saint Augustine I saw that I was not alone in this awareness, this sense of discomfort. It was not something I had imagined. I found a kind of confirmation of my own thoughts and feelings that God must be the One toward whom we constantly journey if our lives are to have real meaning.

Let me tell you, that was a lot for a fourteen-year-old.

I don't remember how many times I've read the *Confessions,* but that doesn't matter. What matters is that in nearly every encounter I have with Saint Augustine's words I gain some new insight. It may not be as dramatic as it was when I was fourteen, but every time I read him deeply, really try to come to grips with what he's saying, I come away seeing things a little bit differently—perhaps a little bit more clearly.

I have read something of Augustine's writings nearly every week for years. There have been long periods of time when I have read him every day. Yet Augustine is that rarest of writers: no matter how many times you have read his words they are always fresh and new. I never feel as if I've absorbed everything he has to say. There is always a new insight around the next corner.

I sometimes marvel at my attraction to Augustine. In certain ways, he and I are very different. For example, I came from a deeply Catholic family and absorbed Catholicism from the very beginning, and I have never felt estranged from the Church. I knew when I was a child I would be a priest, and when I was a teenager that I would be a friar. Augustine, however, had a difficult journey into the Church. As we saw, it took years of vacillation and many fervent prayers from Saint Monica along with the help of Saint Ambrose to make Augustine a Catholic. I can only imagine the turmoil he felt, turmoil that lasted for years. Thinking of the way he struggled and searched, the way he wrestled with his own unruly will year after year before he finally accepted the will of God, seems to me to add even more profundity to the words of his famous quotation. In the depths of his soul he knew what it was to be "restless," and he knew what it was finally to find the "rest" for which his soul yearned—the rest that can be found only in Christ.

I have been a priest for more than fifty years and a psychologist for more than forty. As I look back over my life I realize that my interest in psychology began with my reading of Augustine, for Augustine is one of the great psychologists of all time. His understanding of the human heart and soul is unsurpassed. Interestingly enough, in secular histories of psychology Augustine is sometimes referred to as the "Holy Psychologist," a title he very much deserves. These are the words of a secular author who writes about Augustine's "power as a religious psychologist":

> Augustine had an almost voluptuous sensitivity to the Self in its inner inquietude, its trembling and frailty, its longing to reach beyond itself in love; and in the *Confessions* he gives us a revelation of subjective experience such as even the greatest Hellenic literature does not, and could not, because this interiorization of experience came through Christianity and was unknown to the earlier Greeks.[6]

I would take strong issue here with the word "voluptuous," but not with anything else. Through Augustine's deep encounter with Christ, he became aware, in a way that those before him were not, of the depths of the human psyche—a Greek word that means nothing less than soul. Is it any wonder that in my work as a psychologist I let Augustine be my guide?

As I said before, I am very different from Augustine in many ways; yet his thinking has resonated with me from the beginning. He speaks to me eloquently and powerfully, not only in the *Confessions* but in his great theology, his wonderful devotion to Christ, his magnificent view of creation and of the world around us, and his deep understanding of the mystery and goal of the human soul. One thing that Saint Augustine and I have in common, however, is that neither of us is a natural optimist. Augustine takes a very realistic view of humanity, of sin, of the difficulties of life. Yet through it all, his writings are filled with hope. This hope is not in human things but in Christ's grace and Christ's love for us all. This is the sort of hope that makes sense to those of us who aren't optimists—whether we were born in

Jersey City in the twentieth century or in ancient Carthage many centuries ago.

————

I have pondered long and hard which excerpt of Saint Augustine's writings I should include here. There are literally hundreds of possible choices. Finally I made the decision not to select something deeply philosophical or theological. I have instead decided to introduce you to Augustine the preacher. The following is an excerpt from one of his sermons, which is very appropriately included in the Liturgy of the Hours for Christmas Eve. It is a work of great faith and surpassing beauty.

Awake, mankind! For your sake God has become man. Awake, you who sleep, rise up from the dead, and Christ will enlighten you. I tell you again: For your sake, God became man.

You would have suffered eternal death, had he not been born in time. Never would you have been freed from sinful flesh, had he not taken on Himself the likeness of sinful flesh. You would have suffered everlasting unhappiness, had it not been for this mercy. You would never have returned to life, had he not shared your death. You would have been lost if he had not hastened to your aid. You would have perished, if he had not come.

Let us then joyfully celebrate the coming of our salvation and redemption. Let us celebrate the festive day on which he who is the great and eternal day came from the great and endless day of eternity into our own short day of time.

He has become our justice, our sanctification, our redemption, so that, as it is written: Let him who glories glory in the Lord.

Justified by faith, let us be at peace with God: for justice and peace have embraced one another. Through our Lord

Jesus Christ: for Truth has arisen from the earth. Through whom we have access to that grace in which we stand, and our boast is in our hope of God's glory. He does not say: "of our glory," but of God's glory; for justice has not proceeded from us but has looked down from heaven. Therefore he who glories, let him glory, not in himself, but in the Lord. . . .

For this reason, when our Lord was born of the Virgin, the message of the angelic voices was: Glory to God in the highest, and peace to his people on earth.

For how could there be peace on earth unless *Truth* has arisen from the earth, that is, unless Christ were born of our flesh? And *he is our peace who made the two into one*: that we might be men of good will, sweetly linked by the bond of unity.[7]

SAINT MONICA

I SUSPECT I DON'T HAVE TO tell you that life doesn't always hand us what we want or what we expect. So often we're given situations and people to cope with that seem beyond our power. We work mightily to change things, but nothing happens, or perhaps things even get worse. Those we love head blissfully in all the wrong directions and pay no heed to our warnings—even after disaster strikes. People we care about turn out to be different from what we thought they were—different and not nearly as good. They hurt us so deeply that they seem to tear at our very souls; yet they don't even notice. How does all this happen? Does God accidentally drop us into the wrong family, wrong job, wrong life, or does He just have a very bizarre sense of humor?

For the days, weeks, months, or years when we feel this way, I have a suggestion: Pray to Saint Monica. She's been there.

THE SAINT WHO WOULDN'T GIVE UP

Saint Monica, mother of Saint Augustine, should be the patron saint of family problems or perhaps the patron saint of endurance or perseverance. She was the daughter of an upper-class family in ancient Carthage and was most likely of Berber[1] origins. She was a devout Christian girl, who probably could have had a very normal life if she'd married a devout Christian boy.

Her parents, however, had other ideas and as soon as she was of age gave her in marriage to Patricius, a much older anti-Christian pagan, who was (to put it mildly) not known for his good temper. For years Monica endured her husband's outbursts and more than occasional cruelty. Despite the fact that he denigrated her faith, she prayed for him and worked subtly to bring him to Christ year after year, apparently without much success. Monica never gave up on her wretch of a husband even when all seemed futile. Then finally the unimaginable happened: her prayers were answered and her husband converted. Patricius may have had many faults, but bad timing was not among them. Less than a year after his conversion he was dead. If he is in heaven (or even in purgatory), he has Monica to thank.

Monica and Patricius had three children: Navigius, who was a good son; Perpetua, an exemplary daughter; and the eldest, Augustine, who did everything he could to turn his mother's hair gray before her time. The family didn't have much money and when Augustine was old enough to be sent for advanced schooling, they had to scrimp and save for a while. Because of this Augustine took a year off between his primary schooling and his advanced education, which was to take place in the great city of Carthage. He used this time to read Cicero, which I'm sure Monica thought was a good idea. He also used this time to develop a taste for the sexual excess that was as much a part of ancient Roman civilization as it is of our own. Of this, Monica despaired, as any loving mother would, especially when Augustine produced an out-of-wedlock son at age seventeen.

Perhaps Monica thought that sending Augustine to Carthage would solve the problem of her son's waywardness. It didn't, for once there he lost no time in joining the heretical Manicheans. Since Monica had been working hard for years to get Augustine baptized, this must have been a cruel and agonizing development. Many mothers would have simply given up at this point, but it was not part of Monica's personality to give up—nor was it part of her deep faith. She approached her unruly son's problems the same way she approached her temperamental husband's: with fervent and unrelenting prayer. In the old days Catholics used to use the term "storming heaven." This is a term that was probably invented by Saint Monica.

Monica was not just fervent, she was also strong willed. When Augustine was twenty-nine years old, he announced his plans to leave Africa and go to Rome. Monica was strongly opposed but soon realized that her son could not be dissuaded. Undaunted she decided that if she couldn't stop him, she would go with him to keep him out of trouble. I think we can all imagine how Augustine must have felt when he discovered his mother's plan. Through trickery, he eluded her and set sail with his mistress and little son Adeodatus, leaving Monica on shore. Perhaps she wept at this deception, but not for long, because soon she had booked passage on another ship—not a common thing for a woman alone to have done in ancient times. Monica's voyage across the Mediterranean was apparently not an easy one. The ship was beset by storms, and the crew feared for their safety. It is said that she kept the men from panicking through her calm, her prayers, and her unwavering faith in God.

By the time Monica reached Rome, Augustine had already departed for Milan. So Monica went there, too. It was there that she found her son in the company of Bishop Ambrose, one of the great saints of the early Church and the man who would finally convince Augustine to become a Christian.* Perhaps for the first time in years Monica was able to breathe a sigh of relief.

Like her son, Monica became a friend of Ambrose, who developed a very high opinion of this devout woman from North Africa. Under Ambrose's influence Monica purified her practice of Christianity, abandoning certain quasi-pagan elements that were common in her homeland.[2] She also engaged in many charitable and devotional works while there, earning the admiration of

---

* I confess that I sometimes like to imagine the look on Augustine's face when his determined mother showed up so far from home.

many. It was during this period that Monica's fondest wish was accomplished when Augustine, his heresy and sensual lifestyle now finally behind him, embraced the Church. One can hardly imagine what Monica's joy must have been during the Easter Vigil in which her son was finally baptized by Ambrose. The fulfillment of all her prayers had come about, at last.

It wasn't long afterward that Augustine and Monica, along with Adeodatus and a few others, began the long journey back to Tagaste in North Africa. All went well until they reached the port of Ostia, where Monica fell ill. At first her sickness did not seem severe, but it soon worsened to the point where it was clear she would not recover. Yet Monica was not frightened nor was she sad. She rejoiced that her prayers had been answered, that her son had been reborn for her as a Christian, that through Christ her ties to Augustine could never be broken. As her son stood over her bed she said: "What I have still to do here and why I am here, I do not know. My hope in this world is already fulfilled. The one reason I wanted to stay longer in this life was my desire to see you a Catholic Christian before I die. My God has granted this in a way more than I had hoped. For I see you despising this world's successes to become his servant."[3] Augustine asked her if she was saddened that she would not die in her beloved home but in a land far away. Her answer was typical of this saint. She replied: "Nothing is far from God," and then said she was perfectly happy to be buried wherever she died.

The relationship between Monica and Augustine had been problematic for many years, but in Milan, as Augustine entered the Church, and as Christ became more and more the focal point of his life, their relationship changed. It matured, becoming what a true Christian familial relationship should be. Augustine became profoundly devoted to his mother and genuinely grateful for all she had done for him. He loved her deeply and she loved him with the same intensity. They became, in a way, soul mates.

All of us who have lost our mothers know the intense feelings that this invokes—even in the most devout Christian. So we can understand how Monica's death plunged her family into deep grief. In the *Confessions* Augustine asks his readers for prayers for his parents. It can't hurt to continue praying for Patricius, even after all these many centuries. As far a Monica goes, there is no point in praying for her, but there is every reason in the world to pray *to* her, especially when we despair of our family members or our friends.

In both the Gospels of Saint Matthew and Saint Luke we read Jesus' famous words, "Ask, and it will be given to you." The life of Saint Monica can be looked at as an illustration of those words; for in Monica we have a saint who never stopped asking, who never gave up her trust in God despite the fact that it seemed as if her prayers went unheard. In Saint Monica we have a perfect illustration of the power of prayer and of unwavering trust in God. It took years and years, but Saint Monica's prayers finally bore unimaginable fruit. They brought to Christ a man who would become one of the greatest of the Fathers of the Church, whose thought still guides the Church today.

No Prayers Are Ever in Vain

When I was in Rome several years ago I walked across the street from the Pantheon to the Church of San Augustino. I had never been in that church before, and I was startled to discover that there, next to the high altar, was the tomb of Saint Monica. "Startled" is actually not the right word: "absolutely delighted" would be more accurate. Up to that point I hadn't realized that Saint Monica was buried in Rome, although I was well aware that she had died in Ostia, which is not far from Rome, on her way back to Africa. I knelt down to pray at her tomb and was soon overcome with a profound feeling that I was in the presence of an old friend.

Saint Augustine has been part of my life since my teenage years, and you can't become a friend of Saint Augustine without becoming quite close to Saint Monica, as well. Of course, although I have read a great deal written by Saint Augustine, I have never read anything Saint Monica ever wrote, for there is nothing extant. Yet it's almost difficult for me to believe that fact because I feel as if I know Saint Monica's thoughts and words. It even seems at times as if she has shared her private feelings with me. All this comes through the *Confessions* of her son. In that wonderful book she is lovingly described by a masterful writer, a writer who understood people very well, who was able to see deeply into the souls of others. In the *Confessions* Augustine brings his mother to life for us as he describes his early years with her and his conversion. He is entirely honest and doesn't spare himself or try to make himself into something that he wasn't, so we see the pain that Saint Monica endured because of her son's waywardness. We come to feel the strong urgency that she felt when she looked at the young Augustine, and we become aware of the almost constant prayer that she offered for his conversion. In short, Augustine presents to us a mother's love for her son in a very pure and intense form. It is a generous love that refuses to fade even when it is ignored or rebuffed; it will not give up until the best has been achieved for Augustine. In this sense it is a very Christian love, a love that is totally centered on the good of the one loved, a love that has no ulterior motives or hint of selfishness. The love that Saint Monica has for her son should be a model for all of us in our close relationships with others.

In statues made during the Victorian period and perhaps a little after, Saint Monica is often depicted as an elderly woman[*] carrying a handkerchief. The handkerchief is to indicate that she has been weeping over her son's sinful life. This may seem like a sentimental image, and perhaps it is. Yet there is something here from which we can learn. True Christian love, *agape* in Greek, is a love that is willing to weep, to suffer, to endure hardships for the other. It is willing to tolerate the difficulties and disappointments

---

[*] The fact of the matter is that Saint Monica died at the age of fifty-six, which from my point of view seems the very bloom of youth!

of this life for something much greater than this life. This is the sort of thing that Saint Monica knew well; it was the motivating force in her life. Again, she should be our model as we try to love our family members and friends, many of whom may disappoint us regularly and even greatly.

I am willing to bet that the majority of the people reading this book have, among their relatives, someone (or perhaps several people) who need to be converted. Parents, grandparents, aunts and uncles are often greatly concerned and sometimes even terribly worried about someone in the family who has strayed from the Church. Perhaps such people have not only left the Church but offended us deeply in some other way. Despite what they have done, we know that beneath our hurt and disappointment the old love remains undimmed. We want these people to reconcile with the Church, with us, with the whole family, with God. Over my many years as a priest I have encountered untold people in this situation. My advice varies by the case, but one part of it remains constant. I always tell such people: "Don't waste time. Pray to Saint Monica." This certainly does not mean that we shouldn't pray to Christ Himself or to the Holy Spirit, but it does mean that in Saint Monica we have a friend who has lived through the very problems that we are living through, someone who has seen her own fervent prayers for her son answered but only after many years.

At the end of the ninth book of the *Confessions* Saint Augustine writes in an especially beautiful way about his mother. Here we see the fruit of Monica's prayers. The love that she feels for Augustine is returned; their relationship is healed; all the old problems are gone. This shows what can happen to our human relationships when we permit Christ to be at the center of our lives. It is unimaginable that such a result would have occurred had Augustine not had a true conversion of heart when he entered the Church. This chapter about Saint Monica in the *Confessions* may be unique in the ancient world in that someone of great intelligence and learning gives real honor to a woman. Women were often not written about in the ancient world. So it would be entirely possible that we would know nothing about Monica, that her life would be hidden from us, as were the lives of countless women in her time. Yet we do know about her. In a real sense it is through her prayers, which led to her son's conversion, which led to his writing of her in the *Confessions*, that she has become known to us. We are able to become her friends because she prayed for her son relentlessly, because she loved her son so greatly that she could not bear his being separated from Christ.

━━━━━

Since Saint Monica left no writings for us to examine, we will end our meditation on her with the thoughts of Saint Augustine. This brief excerpt shows the closeness of son and mother, and it also shows what relationships that are healed of all rancor by Christ can become, to what heights they can soar.

The day was imminent when she was to depart this life (the day which you knew and we did not). It came about as I believe by your providence through your hidden ways, that she and I were standing leaning out a window overlooking a garden. It was at the house where we were staying, at Ostia on the Tiber; where, far removed from the crowds, after the exhaustion of the long journey, we were recovering our strength for the voyage.

Alone with each other, we talked very intimately. "Forgetting the past and reaching forward to what lies ahead" (Phil 3:13), we were searching together in the presence of the truth which is you yourself. We asked what quality of life the eternal life of the saints will have, a life which "neither eye has seen nor ear heard nor has it entered into the heart of man" (1 Cor 2:9). But with the mouth of the heart wide open, we drank in the waters flowing from your spring on high, "the spring of life" (Ps 25:10) which is with you. Sprinkled with this dew to the limit of our capacity our minds attempted to some degree to reflect on so great a reality.

The conversation led us towards the conclusion that the pleasure of the bodily senses, however delightful in the radiant light of this physical world, is seen by comparison with the life of eternity to be not even worth considering. Our minds were lifted up by an ardent affection towards eternal life itself. Step by step we climbed beyond all corporeal objects and the heaven itself, where sun, moon, and stars shed light on the earth. We ascended even further by internal reflection and dialogue and wonder at your works, and we entered into our own minds. We moved up beyond them so as to attain to the region of inexhaustible abundance, where you feed Israel eternally with truth for food. There life is the wisdom by which all creatures come into being, both things which are made and will be.[4]

4.

SAINT BENEDICT

WE COME NOW TO BENEDICT of Nursia, a saint whose name is probably familiar to everyone. Yet, paradoxically, he is a saint about whom most people know little. This is a shame because we have all been shaped by Saint Benedict, whether we are aware of it or not. The influence of this saint on the Church and on Western civilization in general is immense. Our great monasteries and religious orders would not be what they are if not for him. Neither would our universities. In fact, if Benedictine monks had not assiduously preserved the great intellectual traditions of Greece and Rome during the Dark Ages, Western culture could not have developed as it did. Saint Benedict is known as "the Father of Western Monasticism," a title he certainly deserves, but he could be called the guardian of Western civilization, as well.

As is the case with many saints of the early Church, Benedict's life is partly obscured from our view. We know more about him than we do about Saint Ignatius of Antioch, but we do not have the wealth of information that we possess concerning Saint Augustine or even Saint Monica; for unlike Augustine, Benedict was not given to the self-analysis that characterized the great North African saint. We are lucky, though, that Pope Gregory I wrote about Benedict in a book titled *Dialogues*. While this is certainly not a biography in the current sense of that word, it is more than a mere character sketch. Although it freely mixes fact with legend, it contains much that is of interest.

So, using this source and the tradition of the Church, let us now take a look at Saint Benedict and find out just why he is among the most honored saints of the Church.

THE SAINT WHO SAVED WESTERN CIVILIZATION

Benedict and his sister Scholastica (who is also a canonized saint) were of noble Roman birth. Tradition tells us they were twins and were born in Nursia (now called Norcia), a small town near Spoleto, Italy, in or around the year 480, about a century after the birth of Saint Augustine. Benedict grew up as the Roman Empire was gasping its last. During his youth the once-stable Italian peninsula was plagued by numerous wars between barbarian tribes and factions. Gloom and uncertainty regarding the future was everywhere; yet Benedict seems to have been protected from this turmoil during his early years. He was educated in Rome and, like others of his class, had the advantage of the best schooling possible for the time. As he neared adulthood, however, he became ever more aware of and disturbed by the immoral lives of his contemporaries. Perhaps desperation and a sense of impending doom propelled people of that time to live licentiously; perhaps it was simply the natural result of the disintegration of a culture, as we may be seeing in our own time. Whatever the case, Benedict found himself simultaneously repelled by the actions of those around him and attracted to them. He constantly compared their way of life with what was taught in the Gospels, and he was acutely aware that in the world around him the teachings of Christ were regularly contradicted or ignored. Probably only in his late teens or very early twenties at the time, Benedict felt pulled mercilessly in both directions. He could easily have given in and become absorbed in all the delights that the world has to offer. Yet Benedict was a young man different from most. His yearning for God was insistent, and this led him to find the grace to turn to Christ rather than to the world. This decision, which I'm sure Benedict viewed as private and personal, would have an impact on generations yet unborn that he could never foresee.

He left Rome, apparently in search of solitude and quiet. It was probably not yet his intention to become a hermit or even a monk, and he certainly had no idea at this point about forming a monastic community. In fact, it seems as if Benedict still had a good deal to learn about renouncing the world, for when he left home he took his old baby nurse as a servant, acting for one last time like the wealthy young man he had been. He settled in a small town called Enfide, which is about thirty miles away from Rome. Soon he was surrounded by a small group of others who were also attempting to retreat from the confusion of the world and to live a life that was concentrated on God.

The way of life of this little community seemed to Benedict very much like the life for which he was searching; yet he began to feel the need for solitude and silence even more intensely. Finally, deciding that what he needed could be found only in complete isolation, he retired to a cave in Subiaco, where he lived the life of a hermit for three years.[1] He spent this time virtually without interruption, devoting his time to prayer and contemplation and doing whatever physical work was necessary. His food was delivered by Romanus of Subiaco, a monk who had encouraged Benedict to make this decision. It was through Romanus that Benedict first received the religious habit.

Apparently Benedict lived an extraordinary life as a hermit, for it wasn't long before word of the prayerful and virtuous recluse of Subiaco began to spread. Soon he was asked by local monks to join them—not simply as a brother, but as their abbot. He was eventually persuaded to take on the duties of abbot, and as soon as he did he declared the place lax and in real need of reform. He was so zealous in his efforts to make the life of the monks more truly religious, that an attempt was made to poison him. Understandably, he returned to his cave.

Despite this, people came to him in increasing numbers, attracted not only by his holiness but because miracles were said to have occurred through his prayers. Soon Benedict was persuaded to start his own monasteries, and eventually he founded twelve of them in and around Subiaco, which became populated by pious men from all walks of life. Later Benedict founded a thirteenth monastery, and this was to become his most famous. The abbey at Monte Cassino is about halfway between Rome and Naples. It became the center of the monastic world. There Benedict went with a group of handpicked monks, and he stayed until his death. It was at Monte Cassino that he wrote his famous rule,[2] which was based partially on earlier monastic writings but largely on his own ideas, things that he had developed over his years as an abbot. This rule became the basis of all Western religious life, the source and bedrock of the monastic tradition. It skillfully balanced work, prayer,[3] rest, the Mass, and all the other aspects of a monastery's life in a very workable and productive way. It was a blueprint for how to live the monastic life in a manner that will bring you ever closer to God. There is an old saying in religious life: "Keep the rule and it will keep you." This is the essence of the Rule of Saint Benedict, a rule that enabled the development of a deep spiritual life, yet did not demand extremes or hardships and was accessible to all.

Benedict's rule affected not only religious life but secular life, as well. It can be considered the first written constitution governing the life of a community, and thus influenced all those who came after it. Not just constitutions of religious orders and other organizations but even the constitutions of nations that came into being centuries after Benedict's death have a debt to pay to him. His rule is the ultimate source of some of their democratic and organizational ideas. The rule also honored and dignified manual labor, an important part of Benedictine life at a time when such labor was often looked down upon.

The Rule of Saint Benedict provided order and a structure for life. It enabled the monasteries to continue to flourish even as civilized Europe seemed to be dying around them. As Europe descended into what some call the Dark Ages, one by one the sources of education and learning disintegrated. Supported by the Benedictine rule, however, the monasteries did not. It was in the monasteries that reading and writing continued, and here a knowledge of Latin and Greek remained common. It was to the monasteries that people hungry for knowledge went, and it was these monasteries that gradually enabled the great universities of the Renaissance to develop.

Saint Benedict died at Monte Cassino in 543 surrounded by his monks. He began his search for God as a very young man and asked nothing more than a closeness to Christ. Yet 1,500 years after his death he is one of the great saints of the Church. He is also the patron saint of Europe and the spiritual father of countless religious communities of men and women. He is a saint to whom each and every one of us owes something.

AN UNDYING LEGACY TO THE CHURCH AND THE WORLD

Most people reading this book are quite aware that I am not a Benedictine. I have never felt called to that way of life, although I admire it greatly, and I have no illusions that I would have been a good monk (although I've been mistakenly called that many times). I'm a friar, and the life of a friar, while bearing some similarities to that of a monk, is different. It is freer in certain respects and not bound to one monastery. The life of a friar is usually centered on some type of apostolic work. Since the day I entered the Capuchins in 1951 I've wanted to work with the poor.

Despite all these facts, I know that I owe my way of life to Saint Benedict, as does every member of every religious community in the Western Church. His concept of *ora et labora*, the balance of prayer and work, is not only at the heart of his rule, it is at the heart of all religious life. His ordering of psalms, canticles and readings into the Divine Office, or Liturgy of the Hours, has enhanced the spiritual life of the Church in a way that is exceeded only by the sacraments themselves. He wisely called this form of prayer—which breaks into the day over and over again, reminding us constantly of the Divine presence—*Opus Dei*, the work of God. It is a beautiful and fitting title. If not for his rule and his many efforts to give form and structure to the religious life, the myriad orders and communities that were founded after his lifetime would never have flourished. Benedict of Nursia did all the groundwork. He constructed the foundation on which the founders of other orders—even Saint Francis—built.

Saint Benedict and his accomplishments have always seemed awe-inspiring to me. He is one of those few human beings who managed to change the course of things in a big way. The Church would never have developed as it did if not for him, nor would European civilization. The form of monasticism he created—or, perhaps we should say, synthesized—was so well grounded, so stable, that it not only survived the destruction of Rome and the Dark Ages but was a virtual beacon of light during them. Western civilization was preserved and nurtured in Benedictine abbeys and so was able to be reborn. The Church was preserved and nurtured in those abbeys, as well. It is possible that some of the great writings of the early Church Fathers would have been lost, at least to the West, for centuries if not for Saint Benedict's devoted spiritual descendants.

It is not hard to see the hand of Providence in all this, although I doubt that Saint Benedict, surrounded by his first followers, thought he was doing anything extraordinary. In fact, I believe that he had only one great desire, and it wasn't to found Western monasticism; it was simply to be close to God. Benedict withdrew from the world to find something that the world lacked. Through this great desire he opened himself up to God in such a way that he became a willing instrument in the hands of the Holy Spirit, and the world was changed.

Few of us are called to the monastic life, and so perhaps we don't see Saint Benedict as a model, but each of us is called to open ourselves to God exactly as he did. We live in a time that, for all its apparent differences, is really very similar to the one in which Saint Benedict lived. He lived as the Roman Empire was in its last stages of disintegration. We live in a time of disintegration, as well. Our culture coarsens a little more each day; abortion is taken for granted; families dissolve at a record pace. All around us we see things crumbling, as did Saint Benedict. We can despair, and the temptation to do so may be strong. Or we can be like Saint Benedict. We can turn from a crumbling civilization to what the world lacks, to the one thing that is capable of giving real stability to our lives—to Christ. If we do this then perhaps we, like Saint Benedict, can make a real difference, perhaps we, too, can become beacons of light in a dark time and build foundations that will last.

If I asked you to imagine what Saint Benedict looked like, I bet you would think of an elderly man with a long white beard—a patriarch. In actual fact Saint Benedict was a young man when he left the clamor and distractions of the world to search for a way of life that was deeper, more satisfying, and more spiritual than any he had known. I don't know about you, but I like that. I like the fact that it was not the wisdom of age which gave birth to monasticism in the West, but the idealism of youth. So, as we think of Benedict of Nursia, it wouldn't hurt to imagine him as a dedicated, earnest, and capable young man with bright dreams of the future and hope for a better way of life. Such thinking is good for someone of my age because the hope of the young is often contagious.

———

The following is a short excerpt from the Prologue of the Rule of Saint Benedict.

Now, brethren, that we have asked the Lord who it is that shall dwell in His tabernacle, we have heard the conditions for dwelling there; and if we fulfill the duties of tenants, we shall be heirs of the kingdom of heaven. Our hearts and our bodies must, therefore, be ready to do battle under the biddings of holy obedience; and let us ask the Lord that He supply by the help of His grace what is impossible to us by nature. And if, flying from the pains of hell, we desire to reach life everlasting, then, while there is yet time, and we are still in the flesh, and are able during the present life to fulfill all these things, we must make haste to do now what will profit us forever.

We are, therefore, about to found a school of the Lord's service, in which we hope to introduce nothing harsh or burdensome. But even if, to correct vices or to preserve charity, sound reason dictateth anything that turneth out somewhat stringent, do not at once fly in dismay from the way of salvation, the beginning of which cannot but be narrow. But as we advance in the religious life and faith, we shall run the way of God's commandments with expanded hearts and unspeakable sweetness of love; so that never departing from His guidance and persevering in the monastery in His doctrine till death, we may by patience share in the sufferings of Christ, and be found worthy to be coheirs with Him of His kingdom.[4]

5.

SAINT FRANCIS OF ASSISI

SAINT FRANCIS OF ASSISI is among the greatest saints of the Church. He is also one of the most attractive—and most challenging. Countless numbers of Christians (and others!) have attempted to imitate him for centuries. Yet in certain ways he is inimitable. During Francis's brief life he established three orders: one for religious men, one for religious women, and one for people who could not abandon their lives in the world. Today there are innumerable groups who claim the name Franciscan and look to Francis as their spiritual father. There is hardly a corner of the world that has not seen a Franciscan.

But who is Saint Francis of Assisi, really? I wonder sometimes if people are able to understand him very well any longer. His radical ideas concerning poverty, for example, are so different from the ways of the world in which we live that perhaps they have become incomprehensible. The world tries to tame Francis, to reduce him to the patron saint of birdbaths, to see him as merely a great animal lover or (more fashionably) as an ecologist. He was far more than that. Let us remind ourselves right away that Saint Francis of Assisi was possibly the most radical Christian the world had seen since the time of the apostles. Saint Francis spent himself totally for Christ. He emptied himself for God and for other people in a way that some might call breathtaking and others appalling. Saint

Francis was the first stigmatist in the history of the Church. He endured the wounds of Christ in his own body, suffering daily with Christ on the Cross. Saint Francis is a saint who knew no compromise with the Faith, who rejected utterly the things of this world, and who was willing to go wherever Christ would lead him no matter what the suffering or consequences. Does that sound to you like the patron saint of birdbaths?

So let's take a fresh look at this great saint, whom I—like so many others—have tried to follow.

THE SAINT WHO GAVE UP EVERYTHING FOR CHRIST

Francis was actually given the name Giovanni (John) at his birth, which occurred sometime in 1181 or 1182 in Assisi, the city with which his name has always been associated. His father, Pietro (Peter) Bernadone, a wealthy cloth merchant, was—for whatever reason—unsatisfied with that name and called his son Francesco, which really means "Frenchman." This name stuck, and for nearly a millennium *il Poverello,* the little poor man of Assisi, has been known by no other name. Francis was doted on by his father. In fact, he was doted on too much, for as a young man Francis became worldly and frankly quite spoiled. By all accounts he had a very charming and winning personality. He was naturally liked, and this enabled him to get away with things that others would not have been able to get away with. All the reports we have of Francis at this stage of his life say that he was something of a dreamer, a boy who was not given to hard work. He liked to enjoy himself, and he also liked to enjoy the good things the world had to offer.

Pietro Bernadone naturally hoped that his son would follow him into the family business, and Francis did make a rather lackluster attempt at this, but apparently that effort did not last very long. When Francis was about twenty he decided to try his hand at a profession far more exciting than that of cloth merchant: he wanted to be a soldier. At that time the military offered plenty of opportunity, as Italy was composed of numerous rival city-states and small principalities. Assisi had embarked on a quarrel with Perugia, a neighboring city, and battle was imminent. One wonders just how much thought Francis put into his decision to don a soldier's armor and risk his life. I suspect not very much. More than likely he had a romantic idea of what war was like and probably was dreaming of glory and adventure. But none of this turned out to be the case. Assisi did not fare well in this conflict, and a good number of prisoners were taken from among their soldiers. Among them was Francesco Bernadone.

In the lives of many saints we can discern a definite turning point, a moment during which their attitudes change, when they perceive things more deeply and see things more clearly. Sometimes this comes all at once, as a moment of great clarity; at other times it happens gradually over a period of time. In Francis's case it was the latter. A year spent in a Perugian prison cell was the beginning of such a great change in Francis's life. I think it is fair to say that he was never the same afterwards. His health was broken in prison, and he probably thought he was going to die. For the first time the careless young man began to question the meaning of his life and to look for a purpose beyond just living day to day, beyond the enjoyment of the moment. In short, he gazed into the abyss of despair, of nothingness, and he didn't like what he saw.

Francis did not die. He was eventually released from prison, and he returned to his family in Assisi both frailer and more thoughtful. They cared for him, even coddled him, hoping to make him once again into the happy youth who had left them a year before. After he regained his health, he did indeed return to the carefree life he had always led, but somehow it was no longer satisfying to him. After a short time Francis realized that another war was in the making, and he decided to search for the glory that had eluded him the first time. The night before he was to leave, however, he had a dream in which he found himself in a huge hall filled with armor that was marked with the sign of the Cross. When he awoke, he was sure that the dream had foretold a bright future awaiting him in the military. He left Assisi but soon fell ill again and had a second dream. In this one he had an overwhelming sense that God was calling him to go home and that it was God's work not the work of war that he was to attend to.

Back in Assisi Francis seemed a different person. He was not yet the saint he would become but he was different. He seemed pushed and pulled between two worlds: the world of the senses and the world of the soul. He tried to find some kind of satisfaction in the life he had always known but discovered himself increasingly alien in this once-familiar world. He left his friends; he stopped wearing his usual fine clothes and put on simpler ones. He made a pilgrimage to Rome, during which he became so disturbed by the small number of offerings at the tomb of St. Peter, that he turned his purse upside down, emptying it on the tomb. Later he gave the very clothes he was wearing to a beggar. Francis then donned the beggar's clothes and spent the rest of the day with the poorest of Rome's poor. Such actions were entirely different from what the world had come to expect of Francesco Bernadone, but they were just the beginning. Not long afterward, Francis encountered a leper. Instinctively he recoiled in horror and fear, but then he stopped and did something that until that very moment would have been totally foreign to him: he embraced the man and then gave him all the money he had. The change that God was working in Francis's soul was progressing nicely.

It was not long after this that Francis entered Assisi's little chapel of San Damiano to pray, a simple act which led to a moment of profound transformation. "Francis, go repair my church, which, as you see, is falling into ruin,"[1] a voice inexplicably coming from the crucifix said. And Francis did exactly as he was told—if a little too literally and impulsively. Without permission, he took his father's luxurious silks and brocades and sold them (along with his own horse) to get money to restore the chapel. Wisely, the priest in charge of the chapel refused the money but did permit Francis to work to repair the structure.

Obviously, Pietro Bernadone was not pleased with his son's latest act. In fact, he was so angry that Francis had to hide in a cave for a month! When Francis finally emerged and made his way back to Assisi, he was so dirty and emaciated that many people made the very reasonable assumption that he had gone stark raving mad. If Francis had hoped that things with his father had improved after a month, he was very mistaken. The once doting Pietro Bernadone was still furious. He dragged the young man home, bound him, and locked him in a closet.

Soon Francis was dragged once again, this time before the Assisi city judges and bishop as his father attempted to force his very strange-acting son to forgo all rights to the family fortune—which Francis was perfectly willing to do. In fact, he was so willing that he gave his father everything he had, including the clothes off his back, every bit of which he took off in the public square. As he did so Francis said to his father: "Hitherto I have called you my father on earth; henceforth I desire to say only 'Our Father who art in Heaven.'"[2] Obviously all this did nothing to change the minds of those who believed that Francis had gone crazy.

Bizarre as this story is, it was a moment of liberation for Francis. He had now severed his ties with his past, with the world of wealth and possessions that had once held him so tightly. He wandered the hills around Assisi, a penniless beggar basking in the presence of God—his new great love. He did his best to fulfill the instructions he had heard from the crucifix as he had understood them, meaning that with mortar and stone he attempted to fix the crumbling little chapels in the area.

During this time Francis heard a sermon on Matthew 10:9 which further transformed him. In this Gospel passage Christ tells his disciples to renounce all worldly possessions and go forth proclaiming the Kingdom of God. Francis had already renounced much. Now the last vestiges of property were discarded. Wearing only the roughest of robes and often barefoot, Francis devoted himself totally to poverty in its purest form. Homeless and carrying nothing, he wandered the Umbrian hills preaching to whoever would listen, and if his words did not move people, his attitude certainly did. Perhaps they could see that this young man who owned nothing was genuinely happy, that he had achieved a kind of peace that riches could not bestow. Whatever the case, within a year, Francis had eleven followers. He welcomed them warmly and formed a small community, which became known as friars minor or "lesser brothers."

The little group of friars expanded constantly, despite the fact that they were almost continually on the move and possessed nothing. In 1209 Francis composed a rule for his followers, which was different from that of the religious orders that preceded him. It expressed his total commitment to poverty and complete reliance on God for all things physical and spiritual.

With his eleven friars and written rule, Francis went to Rome to obtain permission from Pope Innocent III to make his new group an official religious order in the Church. Surely these first Franciscans must have made a strange impression in the eternal city, looking more like vagabonds than monks. The Pope, along with many others, had serious misgivings regarding Francis and his way of life and was planning not to meet with him. Yet a dream—in which Innocent saw the beggar from Assisi single-handedly holding up the Church of Saint John Lateran—changed his mind. The Pope agreed to give Francis's group provisional approval, saying that when God increased the group's numbers, they could return and ask for full approval.[3] This occurred, according to tradition, on April 16, 1210, and that date has always been considered the official founding of the Franciscan order.

Francis returned to Umbria and his preaching, which apparently was quite powerful and convincing for it was attracting new members to his community constantly. It was at about this time that Chiara di Favorone, whom we know as Saint Clare,[4] came to him and the Second Order of Franciscans began. In 1211, or thereabouts,

Francis and his friars finally obtained something like a permanent home. The Benedictines of Monte Subasio gave them the chapel of St. Mary of the Angels, which is also called the *Porziuncola*. Next to this chapel they built some small huts, and this unimposing place became the center of Francis's rapidly expanding order. From the *Porziuncola*, Francis sent his friars two by two[5] out into the world to preach the love of God. These earliest Franciscans must have been quite a sight, journeying from place to place without possessions and seemingly without care. They sang and praised God almost constantly; they either did menial work or begged for their food.

Saint Francis never expected his friars to do anything he was not willing to do, and he went on many preaching expeditions, including one to the Holy Land in an effort to bring the Muslims (not the easiest audience to convince) to Christ. He got as far as the sultan himself (which is a small miracle), who was deeply impressed by the little friar. Francis actually came quite close to converting the sultan but ultimately failed. Despite this he did manage to draw up terms under which the warring Muslims and Crusaders could manage a cease fire. It was approved by the sultan. Unfortunately it was the Christians who turned it down. Even today, however, Franciscans are in charge of the Christian shrines in the Holy Land, and this is a legacy of Francis's visit there.

Success often brings with it unexpected problems, and this was the case as Francis continued to attract enormous numbers of men to his new way of life. Many of them discovered that Francis's uncompromising approach to poverty was too much for them to bear. Many thought it simply impossible—or possible only for a saint—and the strict rules which Francis thought necessary began to be relaxed step by slow step. And this was not the only problem: the order had grown so large that political and ecclesiastical powers thought it should be brought under some measure of control. This again meant straying from the ideals of Francis.

Finally, Francis gave up control of his order and devoted himself to preaching, caring for others, and prayer. Yet by this time, after years living a grueling life, he was different. His will and fervor remained as strong as ever, but his health was now failing and he was nearly blind. He ignored this and continued his usual arduous lifestyle as much as was possible—until he was visited by a new and terrible gift, one which must have shocked him but one which he accepted with joy. In Francis's last years he received the wounds that Christ endured during His last hours: the stigmata. These wounds which mysteriously appeared in Francis's body were, in a certain way, an answer to prayer because Francis had prayed for years to share in Christ's passion. Now, as his own earthly life was drawing to a close, he was given that opportunity, one he accepted as he accepted all that God had ever sent him: humbly and happily.

As Saint Francis's earthly life ebbed he was brought back to one of the huts next to the *Porziuncola*. Here he prepared for his eternal encounter with his Divine Savior. During his last days, although in great and unrelenting pain, he dictated his spiritual testament. On the evening of October 3, 1226, he left all pain behind and entered the unending joy of God's eternal embrace.

Saint Francis of Assisi brings us to the furthest limits of the Christian life. He shows us what total dependence on God really means, what total lack of concern for the things of this world looks like. This amazing saint can at times be frightening and discouraging for us because we know we cannot follow where he leads. Yet we must try to follow him as far as we are able. Each of us can make some aspect of our lives a little like his. Each of us can use Francis as our model as we discard the many impediments our world puts onto our path to God. If we follow Francis—even for a few steps—we will find ourselves closer to God and surely closer to each other.

A Blessed Discomfort:
My Life with St. Francis

I have been a Franciscan for most of my life, and I had developed a strong devotion to Saint Francis long before I ever set foot in a Capuchin-Franciscan monastery. Despite all that, I have a confession to make, and this is something that may surprise you: The fact is that I am uncomfortable with Saint Francis. This has probably always been the case, but I did not become conscious of it until the first time I went to Assisi. As I knelt in the basilica I became very aware of how far short I have fallen in my own attempts to follow in the footsteps of this saint who was so completely dedicated to loving God and man. Without even realizing what I was doing, I started comparing my life with his, and let me tell you, the resulting feeling of inadequacy was overwhelming and haunted me for days. It almost reminded me of the discomfort that I sometimes feel in the Eucharistic presence of Christ, those times when my petty sins and inadequacies make me feel unworthy of His great love. I don't want to imply that I am trying to equate Saint Francis with the Savior, Redeemer and Forgiver of all human beings. Yet there is still something similar that involves a feeling of not having measured up and not having any good excuse for not measuring up.

This was difficult to deal with. It made me feel like a sham, a real fraud. I decided to redouble my efforts to live the Franciscan life in all its simplicity and difficulty. That worked briefly—very briefly—and then I was back in the doldrums of inadequacy. After much prayer and thought I finally came to the realization that except for Saint Clare, almost all the disciples of Saint Francis would—if they were being honest with themselves—feel more or less the way I was feeling because following Francis in all his purity is something that is nearly impossible to do over a lifetime.

The word "seraphic" is used to describe Saint Francis, and I think that is a very good choice of words. A seraph is one of the highest ranks of angels, and to apply this word to a human being—even a saint—is to say something very powerful. It is to say that this person achieved in his human life something that is almost indescribable, something almost celestial. It is to say that Francis reached heights of holiness that we here on the ground floors can't even imagine. In a way, such a term protects us as it reminds us that our imitation of Francis must often be imperfect. Who among us can say that he has lived a seraphic life? Who among us can even say that he has experienced a seraphic moment?

Despite our very human limitations, following Francis can be one of the greatest experiences possible. It opens you up to an acceptance of reality. One of the ways in which it does this is through the door of humiliation. That is something we hate; it is something that our modern world tries to avoid, but humiliation is necessary if we are ever to see ourselves as we truly are. If we try to follow Francis in a sincere way, we will definitely be humiliated, for we will fail over and over again before we have that first blissful moment of success. Francis came to humility easily, but we do not. He therefore offers us ways to gain humility, ways Franciscans of many stripes have been following for hundreds of years. It may take a while, but you learn that being humble in the face of Saint Francis is a very good thing to do. True humility is a gift. It is not really painful and it teaches us to look at ourselves truthfully.

I had a real lesson in humility once as I knelt next to Saint Francis's tomb. I was trying to pray, but prayer did not come easily at that moment; distractions intruded; words turned to dust before I could utter them. I realized my failure and was becoming angry at myself. I wanted to pray at the tomb of Saint Francis. I had planned on it. I had looked forward to this opportunity for months and now it was coming to nothing. Surely Francis himself would never have had this problem, I thought. And then something deep within me reminded me of a truth I sometimes like to forget: I am not Francis. I am not a saint from Assisi; I'm a boy from Jersey City and all I can do is my best. This realization somehow changed things. I continued to kneel but now I was not trying to force prayer from my soul. I found I was simply waiting—but waiting for what? The seconds ticked by and slowly, without any effort on my part, I began to slip into a type of prayer that I did not initiate, a prayer that came from deep within me but really came from outside of me, as well. This prayer had to be humble because it was a gift that could only be accepted in humility. I gradually realized that Saint Francis himself was kneeling next to me, the humble yet seraphic saint who counted himself as nothing and others as everything, the saint who gave one of the more minor of his followers a gift of a few extraordinary moments of prayer—a gift I have remembered ever since.

———

Many of the writings that Saint Francis left behind are letters, short prayers, poems, and fragments. Often his writing seems simple or even simplistic when one first glances at it, but it is not. The following poem—usually called "The Salutation of the Virtues"—is written in a way that will remind you of the famous "Canticle of the Son" (which is also attributed to Saint Francis). It occurred to me that in our virtue-challenged world, these beautiful words of Saint Francis could certainly do no harm and might do quite a lot of good if we would simply take them to heart.

> Hail Queen Wisdom, may the Lord protect you
>   with your sister, holy pure Simplicity.
> Lady, holy Poverty, may the Lord protect you
>   with your sister, Holy Humility.
> Lady, holy Charity, may the Lord protect you
>   with your sister, holy Obedience.
> O most holy Virtues, may the Lord protect all of you,
>   from Whom you come and proceed.
> There is surely no one in the entire world
>   who can possess any one of you
>   unless he dies first.
> Whoever possesses one [of you]
>   and does not offend the others
>   possesses all.

And whoever offends one [of you]
    does not possess any
    and offends all.
And each one destroys vices and sins.
Holy Wisdom destroys
    Satan and all his subtlety.
Pure holy Simplicity destroys
    all the wisdom of the world
    and the wisdom of the body.
Holy Poverty destroys
    the desire for riches
    and avarice
    and the cares of this world.
Holy Humility destroys
    pride
    and all the people who are in the world
    and all things that belong to the world.
Holy Charity destroys
    every temptation of the devil and of the flesh
    and every carnal fear.
Holy Obedience destroys
    every wish of the body and of the flesh
    and binds its mortified body
        to obedience of the Spirit
        and to obedience of one's brother.
and [the person who possesses her] is subject and
submissive
    to all persons in the world
    and not to man only
    but even to all beasts and wild animals
    so that they may do whatever they want with him
    inasmuch as it has been given to them from above
    by the Lord.[6]

SAINT CLARE

I HAVE AN ADMISSION to make: Chiara di Favorone has never sounded to me like the name of a saint. Instead, this beautiful and musical name makes me think of an Italian movie actress or perhaps an opera singer. Yet Chiara di Favorone is definitely the name of a saint—a great Franciscan saint— the one we call Clare in English.

As a Franciscan myself, it is only natural that I'd be partial to Saint Clare, the poor lady of Assisi, and I certainly am. It is no exaggeration to say that she was the greatest of Francis's early disciples and possibly the one who was most similar to him. Clare was so sensitive to the Franciscan spirit, so committed to it, that she has been called *alter Franciscus,* or the other Francis. So let's meet Chiara di Favorone, Clare of Assisi, the beautiful young woman who not only turned her back on a life of luxury to embrace "Lady Poverty" but challenged her entire powerful family to do so— and won.

THE SAINT WHO DISCOVERED WEALTH IN POVERTY

As we just saw, Saint Francis was born into a family of wealthy merchants. Clare, however, came from real nobility. Her father, the Count of Sasso-Rosso, was descended from the Offreducci family, an ancient Roman clan of great prestige. The family of her mother, Ortolona, was also quite venerable, so it was only natural for everyone to assume that Clare, who was the couple's eldest daughter, would marry a nobleman; produce an appropriate number of children; and live a life of wealth, prestige, and ease (as thirteenth-century lives went, that is). In her youth, Clare seemed headed in exactly that direction. Although she was very devout, she probably seemed little different from other girls of her age and station in life. Yet as she approached her later teens something changed; she became reluctant to consider any of the young noblemen who hoped to win her hand in marriage. A strong but vague yearning was beginning to fill Clare's soul—a desire for things beyond this world. In the beginning she may not really have even comprehended that she was being called by God to the religious life, but everything came into focus quite abruptly during the season of Lent when Clare was eighteen years old. It was then that she chanced to hear Saint Francis preach, probably at the Church of San Giorgio in Assisi. It is not certain if Clare heard him once or several times, but that doesn't matter. What matters is that the words of the man in the rough, tattered habit, the man who wore a knotted rope for a belt, changed her way of looking at everything and forever altered the direction of her life.

The elegant Clare lost no time in visiting Francis, to ask for guidance and to express her newfound desire to live exactly the kind of life that he had chosen for himself: the life of poverty, chastity, and obedience; the life of complete self-giving to God and to others. Perhaps Francis was taken aback at first, for although a good number of men had already joined him, Clare was the first woman who had expressed a desire to do so. Whatever his initial reaction, it can be assumed that he quickly saw beyond the fine clothes that this young woman wore, beyond her noble bearing and aristocratic manners. He saw that Chiara di Favorone was different from most, that the same fire for Christ that burned within him had ignited within her, as well. In other words, he recognized her as a kindred spirit, a soul mate. Francis encouraged her, but he was clearly aware of the potential difficulties that would be involved in aiding and abetting a woman like Clare in her plans to leave her family and the destiny they had chosen for her. The two met several times, always in secret. As far as anyone can determine, only two people knew of their encounters: Brother Philip, who accompanied Francis; and Bona, a relative of Clare who always came with the young woman.

Clare was clearly a woman of resolve, and it didn't take her long to make her decision to renounce the world. With Francis's help she did so in a rather theatrical way. Father Boniface Hanley, OFM, who has written about many aspects of Franciscanism, has this to say of her leave-taking:

> On Palm Sunday of the year 1212, while the family was dining, Clare slipped out a back door (tradition says it was the "door of the Dead"—the exit reserved in Umbrian households for the sole purpose of carrying out the family dead), and in the darkness of the night met another kinswoman and accomplice, the Lady Pacifica. The two women then made their way to the chapel of St. Mary of the Angels, where Francis and some of the other friars awaited them. By candlelight, Francis snipped off Clare's long golden tresses. Pacifica slipped a rough brown robe over Clare's feast day dress, fastened it around her waist with a rope, and then covered her shorn head with a black veil. Clare pronounced her vows of poverty, chastity and obedience to almighty God.[1]

And then the problems began. Her family, predictably, was incensed. Perhaps if Clare had decided to join one of the large Benedictine monasteries in the area, they could have come to terms with her decision. Such monasteries had both wealth and prestige, and it is not inconceivable that someone of Clare's intelligence and background would have eventually risen to the status of abbess in one of them. Some people, however, believed Francis to be disreputable and others thought he was simply mad. Whatever he was, the idea that a woman of the Offreducci clan might be in the thrall of a mendicant, a vagabond, was intolerable. Not only that, Clare had the right to her dowry, which was a significant amount of money. Her family feared, with real justification, that if they let her go she would spend it all on the poor. Clare's male relatives—and there were a good many of them—decided to take matters into their own hands and solve this embarrassing problem quickly. They arrived at the Convent of Saint Paul, where Clare was staying temporarily, and demanded that she be handed over to them. When this failed, they forced their way into the convent, determined to accomplish their goal come what may. Father Hanley writes this of what happened next:

> Running to the altar, Clare grasped the altar cloths and refused to budge. When the men succeeded in breaking her grip, she removed her veil and bared her cropped head. The sight of that once beautiful crown minus its golden tresses must have shocked them, for they left her in peace and went back to Assisi. Alone, Clare had withstood her family.[2]

While the family was planning what to do next, their problems worsened. Agnes, Clare's younger sister, stole away and joined Clare in her new life. This only increased the fury of the family, and they decided on yet another assault. Twelve men arrived at St. Angelo's convent, where Clare and Agnes were currently guests. (It seems the nuns at Saint Paul's had had enough.) They found Agnes and grabbed her. Lifting her into the air, they carried her out of the convent, while Clare—still unnoticed by the men but very aware of what was going on—began to pray. The story that has come down to us is that Agnes suddenly became so heavy that the men could no longer carry her and had to put her down. Neither could they lift her up again no matter how hard they tried. All of this proved too much for the men and they finally left, and Clare was at last able to fulfill God's will for her. Thus the Second Order of Saint Francis, usually known as the Poor Clares, began.

From this point on we know rather few details regarding Clare, as is appropriate for one whose life was given over to the cloister and to contemplation. We do know that she and Agnes soon moved to the Church of San Damiano, the very place which Francis painstakingly rebuilt and where he had his mystical experience of Christ, centered on the crucifix which hung there. There they were gradually joined by other women. In the beginning, the new order of Franciscan contemplative women was directed by Francis himself, but within about four years he asked Clare to take over, and almost against her will she accepted. As abbess, Clare was no less decisive than she had been at any other time in her life, and she steadfastly defended her new order from local bishops and other clerics who regularly tried to impose a less rigorous, more Benedictine-like rule upon them. Clare was determined that Francis's intense approach to poverty was the only one that she would follow. When others doubted that women could manage such rigors, she and her sisters regularly proved them wrong.

As I said, we know few facts regarding Clare's later life but we know its general outlines, its broad contours. We also know a number of legends, one of which I want to share with you. It concerns her love of the Eucharist, which—like Francis's—was intense and unwavering. Because of this, statues and paintings of Clare usually show her holding a monstrance. The legend I want to tell you concerns this monstrance. It is said that one time the area in which Clare's monastery stood was under attack, and it seemed clear that the monastery itself would soon be overrun. Clare had the Blessed Sacrament placed in a monstrance above the gate of the monastery and facing the oncoming enemy. She knelt before it and prayed for deliverance. A voice seeming to come from the Host replied, "My protection will never fail you." At that moment the approaching army was overcome with panic and they turned and ran, sparing the convent.

Despite her seeming talent for repelling armies, it is reasonable to assume that Clare rarely—or perhaps never—left the monastery of San Damiano after she first entered it. Be that as it may, she remained Francis's greatest support, always encouraging him, always giving him sound advice. She was the one person who would never fail him when he was in turmoil or doubt. It must have been of great benefit to him to be able to speak to Clare, who saw things so much the way he did. It is Clare who cared for Francis when, blind and weakened by his many austerities, he approached the end of his life; and it is Clare whom we have to thank that Francis never left the apostolic life and turned to the life of contemplation as he was sometimes tempted to do. She counseled him to remain in the world, bringing people to Christ through his works and his words. I'm sure that he saw in her the perfect contemplative that he at times yearned to be and realized that God had given each of them specific tasks that complemented each other perfectly.

Like Francis, Clare wore herself out for God. Her last years were beset by sickness and infirmity, although she struggled on with the help of her sisters. She died when she was fifty-nine, surviving Francis by twenty-seven years. Although a cloistered contemplative, she had become so well known for her holiness that Pope Innocent IV came to visit her as she lay dying, and she had already received the last rites from a cardinal. The passion of John was read to her as she passed from this life into the next, just as it had been for Francis, and her funeral was attended by many from every station in life, from the pope to peasants.

Chiara di Favorone began as a young woman of nobility. As Clare, the Poor Lady of Assisi, she achieved far more than that, she achieved a holiness that can be matched by few. We should see her as a great beacon of light in this world, which is so devoted to acquisition and possession—a sign of contradiction—for in Clare of Assisi we find the perfect example of greatness achieved through sacrifice, through the abandonment of the things of this world, and through a total devotion to the things of God. I am tempted to say that in Clare we find the perfect Franciscan.

The Clarity of Clare and the Beauty of Stillness

Every informed Catholic knows that the life of Saint Francis is filled with beauty, legend, and mystery. There is an almost mystical light that seems to surround this very special saint, a light that can be perceived not only by Catholics but by non-Catholics, non-Christians, and—amazingly—even non-believers. I know of a totally unchurched couple who have displayed a statue of Saint Francis in their front garden for years.

However, we rarely see such statues of Saint Clare, we rarely hear her spoken about. At first glance Clare may seem to be very different from the warm and appealing Francis. She may appear almost austere or even stern compared with him. If you look closer, however, I guarantee that you'll find these differences to be superficial, and you will discover that Saint Clare and Saint Francis are really two of a kind—two different halves of the same whole. The fact that Saint Clare is not nearly as well known as Saint Francis actually befits a contemplative, and we must never forget that Clare was a contemplative to her very core. She is the hidden side of Franciscanism, and as we try to get to know her we must not lose sight of this important fact. It may take some effort to become Clare's friend, but once you do, you see that she has a glow very similar to that of Francis. In my opinion, such a glow is only natural, as this saint's name literally means "clear" or "bright." Clare's clarity, her brightness, I believe, flows from the great simplicity of her life, a simplicity that has enabled her to open her soul to Christ in a very full way. One of the most vital things that Saint Clare teaches us is that holiness, closeness to Christ, is most reasonably achieved by putting aside the things our world prizes most: numberless possessions, the frantic pace at which we all live our lives, the constant chatter that we are all exposed to through the media and Internet. Clare shows us another and better way. In Clare's monastic form of Franciscanism we find a holy stillness, a clear calmness that we do not even see in the same way in Saint Francis. Here we find a subtle and quiet joy that can never be found in the world. We find a closeness to Christ that is extraordinary.

In the little biography of Saint Clare that you have just read, I have tried to describe her accurately, just as I have learned about her over the years. It has been my goal to be as faithful to history as possible. But I have also tried to describe her in the way I have come to know her in my imagination and in my prayer life, for I have prayed to Saint Clare and looked to her for guidance for many, many years.

Saint Clare is important to me because she is a great reminder of what we lack. In her I never fail to see a vital element that our world has missed so regularly and for so long that we have almost forgotten that it could exist. Sad to say, it is often lacking even in the Church. It is certainly, I must confess, frequently lacking in my own over-scheduled life. The life of the Franciscan Friars of the Renewal can be a hectic one. We often find ourselves running from one task to another. As our numbers increase, so, it seems, do our duties. There are so many people in need, so many people who do not know Christ, that the temptation is to work nonstop. But Clare reminds us that this is, indeed, a temptation. Perhaps it may even demonstrate a lack of trust in God, a feeling that all things depend on us. This is never true, and Clare in her silence and her stillness, in her life of intense prayer and intercession, reminds us over and over again that everything really depends on God and our prayerful relationship with Him.

Clare came from a wealthy background, a background of privilege. Yet I believe that there must have been an emptiness, a yearning in the depths of her soul when she was young. I suspect that this was similar to the yearning that pervades our own sad world, the feeling of emptiness that is constantly present in the cluttered lives of so many people. The young Clare possessed a great deal by the standards of her time. Yet she learned early in her life that this was of little meaning. Most of us have yet to learn this, and we waste our lives tying to satisfy the yearning, to fill the emptiness with things, with noise, with entertainment, with chatter. But this never works for long. In the quiet and simplicity of her monastery Clare is perfectly open to the "still small voice" that is God's voice; she is open to filling her life, her whole being, with the love of Christ. In Clare—and in so many of her spiritual daughters, the Poor Clares—we find a kind of joy that we rarely see elsewhere. It is a joy that comes from a truly Christian and profoundly Franciscan non-attachment to things and passing ideas. It is a joy that is anchored in Christ, who is revealed to us once we remove the nonsense that the world prizes. Clare, kneeling in serene prayer before the Blessed Sacrament, has achieved a simplicity that allows her to love Christ and other people with a purity and intensity that are hard to match.

We will close our little mediation on Saint Clare with the words of Pope Innocent IV concerning her. I believe they say what should be said more clearly than any words I could come up with:

> O wondrous blessed clarity of Clare!
> In life she shone to a few;
> after death she shines on the whole world!
> On earth she was a clear light;
> Now in heaven she is a brilliant sun.
>
> O how great the vehemence of the
> brilliance of this clarity!
> On earth this light was indeed kept
> within cloistered walls,
> yet shed abroad its shining rays;
> It was confined within a convent cell,
> yet spread itself through the wide world.[3]

====

Saint Clare did not leave behind a voluminous collection of writings. However, the few things that remain are often beautiful and profound. Her writings basically include four letters written to St. Agnes of Prague, a letter written to Ermentrude of Bruges, the Testament, the Rule, and a Blessing. We shall look at a short extract from one of her letters. I believe that in it we will clearly hear the echo of Saint Francis.

O blessed poverty, who bestows eternal riches on those who love and embrace her! O holy poverty, to those who possess and desire you God promises the kingdom of heaven and offers, indeed, eternal glory and blessed life! O God-centered poverty, whom the Lord Jesus Christ Who ruled and now rules heaven and earth, Who spoke and things were made, condescended to embrace before all else!

The foxes have dens, He says, and the birds of the air have nests, but the Son of Man, Christ, has nowhere to lay His head, but bowing His head gave up His spirit.

If so great and good a Lord, then, on coming into the Virgin's womb, chose to appear despised, needy, and poor in this world, so that people who were in utter poverty and want and in absolute need of heavenly nourishment might become rich in Him by possessing the kingdom of heaven, then rejoice and be glad! Be filled with a remarkable happiness and a spiritual joy! Contempt of the world has pleased You more than [its] honors, poverty more than earthly riches, and You have sought to store up greater treasures in heaven rather than on earth, where rust does not consume nor moth destroy nor thieves break in and steal. Your reward, then, is very great in heaven! And You have truly merited to be called a sister, spouse, and mother of the Son of the Father of the Most High and of the glorious Virgin.[4]

SAINT CATHERINE OF GENOA

SAINT CATHERINE OF GENOA may not be as well known to my readers as some of the other saints in this book. She is certainly not as famous among Catholics as that other great Catherine—Saint Catherine of Siena, who lived about a century before Catherine of Genoa. But I have long considered this saint to be of great importance. She is a mystic; in fact, she is the great mystic of purgatory. It is largely Saint Catherine of Genoa who has formed the contemporary Church's understanding of that interim state that we call purgatory—and, thanks to her, that understanding may be very different and much less severe than you think it is. Saint Catherine of Genoa was also devoted to the poor. Although she was a married woman who never belonged to any religious order, she can be compared in many ways to Mother Teresa in our own time. And that's not all. Saint Catherine of Genoa is that rare Catholic saint who has managed to cross denominational lines. Many Protestants, especially those who have roots in the Holiness Movement, have great admiration for her. They read and even have published some of her writings, although they always call her Madame Adorno, which was her married name. So let's have a look at Catherine of Genoa, a little-known saint whose influence both within the Church and without it is profound.

The Saint Who Saw the Beauty of Purgatory

Caterina Fieschi was born in 1447 in the city of Genoa, with which her name is forever linked. Saint Clare, whom we have already considered, came from an illustrious and noble Italian family, but Catherine of Genoa came from an even higher echelon of society. She was actually related to two popes, Innocent IV and Adrian V; and her father, Giacopo, held the title of Viceroy of Naples, a position of great importance. As a girl and the youngest of five children, Catherine's marriageability was seen as her greatest asset, and at the age of sixteen she was wed (much to her dismay) to Giuliano Adorno in an effort to end a long-standing feud between her family and his. Like many arranged marriages this one had its problems: Giuliano quickly proved to be unfaithful, ill-tempered, and even inclined toward violence. He was also such a lavish spender that he seemed certain to squander his entire huge inheritance. Catherine, who in her girlhood had dearly wanted to become an Augustinian nun, found herself instead as a married woman living a life similar to Augustine's mother, Saint Monica. She was, in short, miserable, and for the first five years of married life suffered in silence. She withdrew into herself, succumbing to depression and becoming nearly a recluse. For the next five years, Catherine attempted to find some pleasure in the good things that the world has to offer, but she eventually realized that these could bring her no lasting happiness. She became so desperate that she actually prayed for illness just so that she could live a life of seclusion, but these prayers were not answered.

After about ten years of this Catherine probably felt as if there were no possible way out of her situation. Her older sister, who had entered the Augustinian convent to which Catherine has aspired, advised her to go to confession to the sisters' confessor, which Catherine did—or at least she tried to go to confession. She made her examination of conscience, entered the confessional, and knelt down. Almost immediately Catherine began to experience herself, the world around her, God—everything—

differently. Inexplicably, she was overwhelmed by, flooded with, the love of God—the same God who had begun to seem distant and perhaps even uncaring to her in her suffering. Her own sinfulness also became crystal clear to her for the first time and with it a great—almost overwhelming—desire for repentance. All this was too much for the young woman, and she collapsed to the floor of the confessional, perhaps in a faint, perhaps in some kind of ecstasy. Caterina Fieschi Adorno was never the same again.

Although it is doubtful if Catherine had experienced any real contact with the poor up to this time, she was suddenly seized by a need to help those who had little. Soon she was regularly making her way into the slums of Genoa to help the sick and to bring food to those who had none. Such work could not have been easy; the squalor and the sickness must have been overpowering and even repulsive to one raised as Catherine of Genoa had been, but she continued, and at the same time she began to develop a prayer life that deepened constantly. She also developed a life of real penance that included long fasts[1] and much self-denial. In short, this young woman, who seemed to have been slightly shallow, self-absorbed, and self-pitying up to this point, began to live a life completely given over to God and to others. During this period, her husband, Giuliano, finally accomplished the inevitable: he ran through the last of his money and went bankrupt, a great disgrace and terrible humiliation in Genoa at that time.

Perhaps it was the shock of losing his fortune or perhaps it was his wife's example, but in a very few years Giuliano, too, underwent a conversion, becoming a Franciscan tertiary.[2] He soon began to help Catherine in her work with the poor. In 1479 the couple, who had begun their marriage miserable but living in a palace, now were feeling a sense of peace and happiness, although they had no choice but to move into very modest quarters. They decided to live near the Pammatone Hospital, which was for the poor of Genoa, and the two of them worked there for many years with great devotion and without any pay at all.

In 1490, Catherine became the director of the hospital. She took her new position very seriously and worked diligently to improve conditions. Three years later she was making great headway when the bubonic plague broke out in Genoa, causing devastation and terrible panic. Many people fled the city, knowing that remaining was likely to cost them their lives. Catherine and her husband could have left, but they stayed at the hospital, doing all that was in their power to help the afflicted. Eventually eighty percent of the population who remained behind died. Among them was Giuliano, although Catherine herself almost miraculously remained unaffected by the terrible disease. She eventually resigned her position as director of the hospital but continued working there almost without rest until eventually, her health began to deteriorate.

Catherine lived little more than ten years after leaving the Pammatone Hospital. During this time the mystical element of her life, which was always powerful, came to dominate. Penance and reparation for sins had always been a primary focus for her, and this led naturally into long meditations on purgatory, which some people have not hesitated to call private revelations. She wrote about this in a book called *Trattato del Purgatorio* (Treatise on Purgatory). Revolutionary at the time and still very different from the understanding of many Catholics, this book characterizes purgatory as a state of joy rather than one of suffering. Many Catholics still conceive of purgatory as a kind of temporary hell, but for Saint Catherine of Genoa it is a state of gentle and constant healing, a rebuilding of the soul to make the soul suitable for its eternal encounter with Christ. One of the most famous lines from the *Treatise on Purgatory* sums up her ideas perfectly: "There is no joy save that in paradise to be compared to the joy of the souls in purgatory"[3] Saint Catherine of Genoa's ideas concerning purgatory have had a great impact on the Church and, primarily for that reason, there is speculation that she may one day be named a Doctor of the Church.[4]

She also wrote the *Dialogo Spirituale tra anima e corpo* (A Spiritual Dialogue between the soul and the body), which shows a different yet no less mystical side of Catherine. This book is a profound yet witty conversation between the soul and the body, which really tells of the conflicts and difficulties Catherine underwent as her spiritual life developed.

By the time Catherine reached her early sixties she was exhausted but exultant. She was nearing the end of her life and she knew she would soon leave this world and enter eternity. Yet in a sense it seemed as if she were already in heaven. Although she suffered many physical pains, her mystical experiences steadily deepened, opening up a world to her that few of us can imagine.

Catherine of Genoa died in 1510, leaving behind her a legacy that is still with us. She is a saint who at times is difficult to comprehend, a saint of many austerities, yet she is the saint who, almost more than anyone else, has taught us of the overwhelming love of God that is poured out to us, healing us of our sins and bringing us ever closer to Him.

THE SAINT ON THE WALL:
SAINT CATHERINE OF GENOA

In my combined office/bedroom at Trinity Retreat most of the walls are lined with shelves on which sit the books I've been collecting for decades. There's not much wall space other than that, so I don't have many pictures. One picture I do have—one I insist on having—is a reproduction of a portrait of the saint we are now considering, Saint Catherine of Genoa. She has become an extraordinarily important saint to me over the years. However, unlike Saint Thérèse, whom I encountered when I was a child, I did not meet Saint Catherine of Genoa until I was already an adult. I suppose I had heard her name from time to time, but I did not really know anything about her until I was a graduate student in psychology. It was then that I discovered a magnificent work titled *The Mystical Element of Religion* by Baron Friedrich von Hügel. This book treated Catherine of Genoa in great detail, and the more I read, the more fascinated I became. I didn't realize it then but I was beginning a friendship that would last for the rest of my life.

Saint Catherine of Genoa was a mystic, and this is something that greatly attracted me. Her mysticism focused on the great Catholic doctrine of purgatory, that interim state of purification the soul undergoes after death and before entrance into the eternal encounter with Christ that we call heaven. I grew up at a time when, for various reasons, purgatory was still thought of as a place of terrible torment, a place where purification is effected only through pain and suffering. I remember frescoes painted around the domes of some Catholic churches that were supposed to represent purgatory. They usually showed the Blessed Mother or Christ reaching down into a pool of what looked like blazing oil and pulling a soul out of its agony and into the joys of heaven. It almost seemed like taking a turkey out of the oven when it was done.

I hadn't completely realized it as I was first learning about Catherine of Genoa but something in me was looking for a fuller, deeper understanding of purgatory, and I certainly found this in the writings of this wonderful saint. Here I encountered an understanding of purgatory that made it seem like a gift given to us out of love rather than a punishment from a stern and angry God. As soon as I read her words, I realized that Catherine of Genoa must have it right, for hers was a vision that included God's boundless love rather than merely concentrating on God's justice or wrath. It was truly Catholic. It was a full vision of purgatory, and in reading Catherine of Genoa I really understood the Church's teaching on purgatory for the first time, and I think I understood God's love for us in a deeper way, as well.

Saint Catherine of Genoa also intrigued me because she combined a strong mysticism with an equally strong compassion for the poor and the ill. The work she did in the Pammatone Hospital in Genoa was truly selfless. She reminds me over and over again that the life of a Christian is not a life that chooses either contemplation or the active apostolic life. The life of the Christian embraces both, and each renews and strengthens the other.

I am now seventy-eight years old, and I have spent all but my first seventeen years in the religious life. I have also spent over fifty years as a priest. At times, if you don't watch out, this can lead to a rather biased understanding of things. Perhaps a person with my background might be tempted to see in the religious life and the priesthood a superior form of life. Perhaps such a person would be tempted to look at all the great priests, nuns, and brothers and see them as God's unique instruments. Here again Saint Catherine of Genoa comes to the rescue. She was a laywoman who accomplished amazing things for the Church at a time when laywomen had very little power. Catherine of Genoa can save a priest or religious from pride and arrogance, for in her time she probably accomplished more than all the clergy of Genoa put together. This is also the element that made Saint Catherine of Genoa palatable (if I may use that word) to Protestants. They simply couldn't understand a person like Saint Teresa of Avila or Saint Thérèse of Lisieux. The cloistered life is too foreign to the way traditional Protestants think. But a married woman like Saint Catherine of Genoa was another story. Her life was comprehensible to them and perhaps, through her, Catholicism became a little more comprehensible to them, as well.

I will never forget the day I visited Genoa and entered the church where her body can be seen next to a side altar. Of course I knew what she looked like from the portrait on my wall, but I was very surprised to see that she is very recognizable after five hundred years. I think that the time is not too far off when I shall meet Saint Catherine of Genoa in a different way. I am an old man now and most of my life on earth is over. I have certainly not accomplished what Saint Catherine of Genoa accomplished, but with the aid of her prayers and those of many other saints, I believe I have not done too badly. When the time comes I will face my inevitable stay in purgatory not with fear and trepidation but with hope and expectation. And I will thank this wonderful saint who has taught me that purgatory is truly an expression of the limitless love of God.

———

The following is a small excerpt from Saint Catherine of Genoa's Treatise on Purgatory. *I suspect that if you compare it with your own understanding of purgatory, you will find it much more full of the love of God.*

These souls cannot think,
"I am here, and just so because of my sins,"
or "I wish I had never committed such sins
for now I would be in paradise,"
or "That person there is leaving before me,"
or "I will leave before that other one."
They cannot remember the good and evil
in their past nor that of others.
Such is their joy in God's will, in His pleasure
that they have no concerns for themselves
but dwell only on the their joy in God's ordinance
in having Him do what He will.
They see only the goodness of God,
His mercy toward men.
Should they be aware of other good or evil
theirs would not be perfect charity.
They do not see that their suffering
is due to their sins
for that awareness would be a want of perfection
and in purgatory souls cannot sin.
Only once do the souls understand
the reason for their purgatory: the moment in which they
    leave this life.

After that moment, that knowledge disappears.
Immersed in charity, incapable of deviating from it,
They can only will or desire pure love.
There is no joy save that in paradise
to be compared to the joy of the souls in purgatory.
This joy increases day by day.[5]

8.

SAINT THOMAS MORE

BY NOW WE SHOULD ALL BE aware that saints come in a variety of sizes and shapes. There is no one personality type or one pattern of life that is common to those who have achieved real sanctity during their earthly lives. The secular world often imagines saints as if they are cut from a single mold—or at least a couple of molds: saints either have to be so spiritual that they have trouble keeping their feet on the ground or they are relentlessly pious do-gooders. Such ideas are one-dimensional; they forget the human element, the extraordinary variety possible in human life, and suggest that saints are a different breed from the rest of us. Nonsense! I hope that if you have read this far, you have realized that saints are real people with real lives. Sanctity can take root in almost any life that is not given over to sin. It is what God has created us for, after all. Any one of us, if we cooperate with the graces that God so abundantly bestows on us, can become a saint, even if we must remain entrenched in the difficulties of real life in this very difficult and frustrating world.

The saint who we will now examine was just such a man. Thomas More was a writer, a philosopher, a lawyer, a statesman, and a personal friend of the Renaissance thinker Erasmus. More held high government office and often was forced to balance the demands of his position with the demands of his faith. He was a man of immense internal strength and a profound sense of right and wrong. At the end of his life he did what few people around him were able to do. He firmly put his faith in God rather than in a king who wanted to usurp the place of God. This was a decision that propelled Thomas More toward tragedy, a tragedy he understood very well and yet accepted. It was also a decision that propelled him toward a sanctity that can have no end.

THE SAINT WHO SAID "NO" TO A KING

Born in London in February of 1478, Thomas More seems to have had his profession at least partially dictated to him from his earliest years. His father Sir John More, a successful lawyer, was utterly dedicated to the law and determined that his son follow him into what he considered a noble profession. Thomas was educated at the best schools in London and all reports suggest that he was a superior student with a penetrating mind. Even as a small boy he excelled, and when he was twelve he was selected to be a page for the Archbishop of Canterbury, an important honor, indeed. The archbishop thought so much of his page that two years later he paved the way for More to begin studies at Oxford University, even though the boy was not yet fifteen. At Oxford More studied Greek and Latin as well a French, history, and mathematics. He was also exposed to the new ideas of the Renaissance that were flowing through Europe at that time, invigorating its universities and offering a new humanistic approach to learning. After two years he left the university at his father's insistence to begin legal training in London, and in 1502 his legal career began.

All during this period More's spiritual life was growing at least as much as was his intellectual life. In his late teens and early twenties he started spending as much time as he could at the Charterhouse[1] outside London. There he participated in the prayer life of the monks and took on some of the austerities that characterized monastic life—practices that would stay with him for the rest of his life. He very seriously considered entering the monastery but finally chose instead to remain in the law, believing that God's call to him was to be a Christian layman. At the age of twenty-six he won election to Parliament, and the next year he married a young woman named Jane Colt. Finding that his new wife's education had been somewhat neglected (as was the custom of the time) More did what few husbands then would have done: he became her teacher, introducing her to literature, music, and philosophy. The couple eventually had three sons and one daughter. It was then that real misfortune struck the life of Thomas More for the first but certainly not the last time. In 1511, his wife Jane died. Despite his sorrow at her loss, and knowing that his children must have a mother, Thomas soon remarried Alice Middleton, a wealthy widow.

Today we might say that Thomas More was on the fast track. In 1510 he was appointed as one of the two undersheriffs of London. In this position, which carried much responsibility with it, he successfully managed to blend his characteristic legal impartiality with a great kindness for the poor. In 1515 he accompanied an important delegation to Flanders to help negotiate a settlement to some disputes about the wool trade. In 1517 he was essential in stopping an uprising in London aimed at foreigners. His accomplishments were many, and he was more than noticed by King Henry VIII, who made him a member of his Privy Council (the king's closest advisors) in 1518. Thomas was knighted by Henry in 1521.

We usually think of King Henry VIII as old, fat, and in the habit of either divorcing or beheading a long series of wives. We also tend to think of him as the cause of England's separation from the Catholic Church. While none of this is untrue, the Henry VIII of the early 1500s was very different from these images. He was an earnest young man in his thirties, and a devout Catholic who was very concerned about the spread of Lutheranism on the European continent. Henry wrote *Defence of the Seven Sacraments*, which refuted Lutheran theology so well that Pope Leo X granted the king the title "Defender of the Faith," a designation that British monarchs still use today. It is assumed by many that Thomas More helped the king in the writing of this book, that many of the ideas in it were really his. When Luther replied to the work, it was Thomas More, under a pseudonym, who deftly answered him. All this greatly impressed Henry, who drew More closer and closer to him. The king could see More's talent and knew he was a man to trust. He made More Speaker of the House of Commons in 1523 and Chancellor of the Duchy of Lancaster in 1525.

In 1529 King Henry dismissed Cardinal Woolsey as his Lord Chancellor (the highest position in the government) and appointed Thomas More—the first layman ever to hold this post. As such Thomas More became the most powerful man in England after the king. Yet it was at this time that his undoing began, for he realized more and more that the king was moving in a direction in which he could never follow. Henry, in need of money, was becoming increasingly willful and was eyeing property owned by the Church and especially the monasteries. He would soon decide to take most of it for himself. At the same time, obsessed with having a son and heir, Henry was attempting to annul his marriage to Catherine of Aragon, whom he believed could never provide him with such an heir. When Rome refused the king's annulment, the die was cast; and Henry VIII, once the "defender of the faith," declared himself "Supreme Head of the Church." The man who had once powerfully opposed the Protestant Reformation now began to take actions that would put him in the forefront of it. All this appalled Thomas More and caused him to submit his resignation—which the king refused.

The king made one step after another to separate England from the Church. More approved of none of them but could not stop his monarch, despite his own high position. Henry, used to having anything he wanted, believed he could have Thomas, too, and could bring him around to support his actions. He was very wrong. Thomas More stood firm. One by one, bishops and priests, earls and barons, declared their allegiance to Henry as head of the

Church in England. More however, steadfastly refused, despite the fact that, increasingly, he stood alone. Surely he knew the risks he was taking and what the result of his refusal must eventually be. Yet he remained a Catholic and firmly loyal to the Pope. A man of profound devotion to Jesus Christ, Thomas More embarked on a road that was destined to lead to earthly disaster. In essence, he knew that this was the road to Calvary, but he also knew that he was walking it with Jesus, and this is what sustained him.

Eventually Henry's patience was at an end. He permitted More to resign as Chancellor. With this resignation Thomas More lost all his property and nearly all his income. The once powerful man was reduced to a kind of genteel poverty and quiet ostracism.

The year 1533 was a decisive one for England and a fateful one for Thomas More. That was when Henry VIII, his self-granted annulment final, married his second wife, Anne Boleyn. Thomas More refused to attend the coronation of the new Queen of England, a refusal that infuriated the king, who (probably quite rightly) interpreted More's act as a statement of the illegitimacy of his new marriage. The king took action.

Trumped up charges were made against More. One accused him of taking bribes, another of attempting to interfere in state matters. Brilliant lawyer that he was, More disposed of both charges easily, but this certainly did not assure his safety. In 1534 he was commanded to swear his allegiance to the parliamentary Act of Succession (which made Boleyn queen and any children of her marriage to Henry VIII heirs to the throne). More avoided this problem deftly by stating that it was Parliament's right to make anyone they chose part of the royal succession. Then he faced another demand, one that would prove fatal. He was commanded to take the oath of supremacy, which stated that Henry, not the Pope, had supreme power over the Church in England. Although he knew the consequences, he remained silent.

More was arrested and sent to the Tower of London. Many people continued to urge him to take the oath and save himself. He did not. He was charged with high treason and tried. He defended himself well but was finally convicted on what was surely false evidence. He was sentenced to be hanged, then drawn and quartered, but the king—in a moment of kindness toward the man who had done so much for him—commuted this sentence to simple beheading.

In the Tower of London, awaiting execution, Thomas More turned to what had sustained him throughout his life: devotion to Christ. He began work on a book entitled *De Tristitia Christi* (*On the Sorrow of Christ*), which I have often called one of the most important books in the history of devotion. It is a book that draws the reader into a deep contemplation of the Passion of Christ. This work is even more astounding when one realizes that it was written during a time when More was deprived of all books. Its many quotations from Scripture were written completely from memory—and they are perfect. Here we find More accepting his cross in profound faith and trust, in true union with Christ.

On July 6, 1535, Thomas More was beheaded. He went serenely and even cheerfully to his death—a death he could have avoided up to the last minute by accepting Henry as head of the Church. Perhaps such a statement could even have given him back his property and position, but he would not—could not—make it. He could not deny the Church as he knew Christ had established it.

In Thomas More we have a hero saint, a man who put Christ above everything, even his own life. Few among us are called to sacrifice what Thomas More sacrificed, yet his strength and courage in resisting the idols offered by the world should inspire us all. Often we are tempted to make compromises in our faith; often the world tells us that the Church is wrong, that Christ Himself is wrong, that the Church is outdated and should constantly adapt to the whims of the world. Such ideas are often tempting, but when we hear them we should remember Thomas More, a saint whose devotion to Christ and to the truth was so great that compromise was unthinkable.

The Courage to Say "No" to the World

At first glance we may think that the dramatic life of Thomas More, while very moving and exciting, has little to teach us. We are, after all, not likely to have much to do with kings, and the chances of any of the readers of this book ending their lives by being beheaded for treason is—blessedly—infinitesimally small. So, we must look further and deeper to see what this saint really reveals to us.

One of the things that has always most impressed me about the life of Thomas More is that he was a layman, a layman who stood firm for the Church during a time when cardinals and bishops—not to mention the rest of the clergy—were jumping ship en masse. Often, as Catholics, we tend to assume that our priests and religious should be on a spiritual level that is different, higher than the rest of us. We are bitterly disappointed and even angered when we discover that this is not always so. Priests and religious are just as afflicted by original sin as everyone else, as our own recent history shows so well and so sadly. Thomas More reminds us in no uncertain terms that the Church does not depend totally on the ordained or on those who have taken religious vows. He reminds us that God is just as liable to raise up a great saint among the laity as among the clergy.

Saint Thomas More is a saint who displays a rare kind of courage. It is a kind of courage that is hardly seen in our culture anymore, and it is a kind of courage that fascinates me. Perhaps we can call it the courage of refusal, the courage to say "no" to the world, to all the powers of the world, to the society in which one lives, to ideas that have taken root and are accepted but are nonetheless wrong. The courage of Thomas More was a courage that did not consider the cost. It was totally centered on God and truth. It looked to eternity for its foundation, giving little thought to the passing ideas of the moment.

Thomas More was faced with a drastic choice between God and his king, which really meant between God and the country that he loved and had served so well. As I think of him facing this decision, I imagine that he saw this choice in stark terms. I believe that he saw the two paths open to him as being between God and idolatry. When Henry proclaimed himself the head of the Church in England he set himself up as a kind of idol, a secular monarch who usurped the place of the Vicar of Christ—and therefore of Christ Himself. Thus he was essentially saying that the secular world has the power to decide or even dictate the will of the Church or even of God. This Thomas More knew to be profoundly wrong, to strike at the very heart of Christianity. Although almost everyone around him seemed to acquiesce to this, Thomas More had the courage to say "no."

We, too, live at a time when the secular world demands the right to dictate the will of God. We live at a time when secular courts decide that unborn children are not people. We live at a time when marriage is declared to have no intrinsic nature, when it can be changed in any way that the majority of us want it to be changed. We live at a time when we are told there is no such thing as the natural law, that the only meaning that exists is the one we impose on a meaningless universe. Such subjective meaning can be changed at will or even on a whim. In our time secularism is deified in a way far clearer than it was in Thomas More's time. We feel that we have inexplicably become the minority, that the voice of Christians is no longer heard or, if it is heard, it is not respected.

In our difficult times I believe there is no saint whose life is more worthy of meditation and emulation than Saint Thomas More. I think of him often and pray that I will be granted a small shred of the courage he displayed. He is the saint who can teach us to say "no" to those things to which we must say "no." He is the brave and brilliant saint who teaches us to proclaim the truth even if the cost of doing so should be no less than everything.

Thomas More died a traitor to his king but a saint to God. I'm sure those who participated in his trial and execution believed his memory could easily be blotted from history. Instead he has become one of the most admired men of Western civilization. I remember some years ago the Anglican vicar of the Church of Saint Peter in Chains at the Tower of London volunteered his opinion to me that Thomas More was the greatest man whose bones rest in the ossuary under the church. I agree with him, and I believe that Saint Thomas More's greatness rests on his realization that sometimes we must say "no" to the world in order to say "yes" to God.

———

The following is from Saint Thomas More's great unfinished work, De Tristitia Christi. *As you read this, meditate on the fact that this was written as More prepared for his own execution. Contemplate how he drew on Christ's passion and death to give himself the strength to endure his own trials.*

O saving Christ, only a little while ago, you were so fearful that you lay face down in a most pitiable attitude and sweat blood as you begged your father to take away the chalice of your passion. How is it that now, by a sudden reversal, you leap up and spring forth like a giant running his race and come forward eagerly to meet those who seek to inflict that passion upon you? How is it that you freely identify yourself to those who openly admit they are seeking you but who do not know that you are the one they are seeking? Hither, hither let all hasten who are faint of heart. Here let them take firm hold of an unwavering hope when they feel themselves struck by a horror of death. For just as they share Christ's agony, His fear, grief, anxiety, sadness, and sweat (provided that they pray, and persist in prayer, and submit themselves wholeheartedly to the will of God), they will also share this consolation, undoubtedly they will feel themselves helped by such consolation as Christ felt; and they will be so refreshed by the spirit of Christ that they will feel their hearts renewed as the old face of the earth is renewed by the dew from heaven, and by means of the wood of Christ's cross let down into the water of their sorrow, the thought of death, once so bitter, will grow sweet, eagerness will take the place of grief, mental strength and courage will replace dread, and finally they will long for the death they had viewed with horror, considering life a sad thing and death a gain, desiring to be dissolved and to be with Christ.[2]

9.

Saint Teresa of Avila

WE COME NOW TO an absolutely fascinating saint, Saint Teresa of Avila. A mystic of great depth, she was also a reformer of great power and a contemplative with a charming and remarkably robust personality. Here we find a woman who was daunted by nothing—at times, it seemed, not even by God. There is a famous story about her that I love, which tells of her making a visit to one of the monasteries she founded. On her way her horse started bucking, depositing the saint in a stream. Picking herself up, Saint Teresa is reputed to have looked at the heavens and said to God: "If this is the way you treat your friends, it's no wonder you have so few of them!" Is this story true? Perhaps, but whether it is or not, it tells us something that is very true about this wonderful saint. It does not, however, come close to telling the whole story, for that soggy saint standing in the stream is the same woman who wrote the following words:

> Let nothing disturb you,
> Let nothing frighten you.
> Everything passes;
> God never changes.
> Patience obtains all.
> Whoever has God wants for nothing;
> God alone is enough.

These few spare phrases convey an astonishing amount. They cut right to the heart of the matter, to the ultimate depth of our lives. They sweep aside our countless preoccupations, the endless little idols we prefer to the true God, and confront us with the meaning of our existence in an absolutely truthful and unvarnished way. These are words that in their simplicity and power could only have been written by one whose knowledge of and trust in God was extraordinarily profound.

So let us take a look at the life of this very remarkable saint, this Doctor of the Church and spiritual writer. Here we will meet a woman who called herself a "worldly nun" and who had great trouble praying for her first two decades in religious life. Yet she is the same woman who became one of the greatest guides in the art of prayer the world has known.

THE SAINT WHO COULDN'T PRAY

Teresa de Cepeda y Ahumada came into this world, as did so many of the saints we are considering in this book, as a member of a large family. One of ten children born to her parents, she also had two older half-siblings, for her father had been married before and widowed. Saint Teresa's father, Alonso de Cepeda, and her mother, Beatriz de Ahumada, were members of the gentry class but were by no means part of Spain's upper nobility. Nonetheless their children enjoyed a standard of living that was better by far than that of most people.

The determination and inventiveness which marked Saint Teresa's life was very much in evidence from her earliest years. When she was only about seven years old she convinced her older brother Rodrigo that the two of them should leave home together. Lest you think there was nothing unusual in this, as many children decide to run away from home at one point or another, let me tell you her reason. In her own words the point was to "go off to the land of the Moors and beg them, out of love of God, to cut off our heads there." In other words, at the age of seven she decided that the time was ripe to become a martyr. Of course the two children didn't get very far before one of their uncles found them and brought them home. Martyrdom had been averted, as had the long trip to Africa, for God had great plans for this little girl and they didn't include being beheaded by the Moors or anyone else.

Teresa's father was a devout but very strict man. Her mother, also very religious, was more lenient in her approach to child-rearing. It is probable that because of her outgoing nature and warm personality, Teresa was her mother's favorite, making the girl feel both loved and secure. That, however, was not to last very long. By the time the saint-to-be was fifteen years old, her mother died, leaving Teresa bereft and unsure of the future. When confronted with this loss, Teresa's strong faith immediately took over, and she turned to another mother to replace the one she had lost. She later wrote: "With many tears I implored the Holy Virgin to become my mother now." From that point onward, Teresa had a great devotion to and a perfect trust in our Lady.

As I'm sure many of us remember, the teen years are rarely the time when religious or spiritual concerns are in the forefront of our minds. During that time of life we are thrilled—even intoxicated—with our newfound freedom. Our gaze is turned outward to a world that has just opened up to us and seems to hold endless promise. This attitude is one to which even future saints can fall prey. And so during her adolescence (her childhood desire for early martyrdom forgotten) Teresa became a rather worldly young woman, interested in beautiful clothes, the finer things that Spanish life had to offer, and dashing young Spanish men. Her outgoing and charming personality provided her with a wide circle of friends. She was what we might call "popular." All this plus Teresa's sudden interest in books of chivalry (the closest things to romance novels that existed at the time) proved too much for her strict father to endure, and the next thing Teresa knew was that she had been packed off to an Augustinian convent.

There she encountered the religious life for the first time, and although she did not stay at the convent for more than a year and a half due to illness, this worldly young girl was changed in some important way—put back on the right track, we might say. Later, when she was once again at home, a reading of the Letters of Saint Jerome convinced her that she was being called by God to the life of the cloister. Her father, however, would have none of it, so Teresa—not one to be easily thwarted—left home on her own and made her way to the Carmelite Convent of the Incarnation at Avila. This move proved to be far more difficult than Teresa had anticipated and she later wrote that being separated from her family gave her a sense of loss so great that it was like a death. But she stayed and persevered, although at that time the convent was not living a very strict Carmelite life and, in fact, had become very lax. In this environment Teresa worked to develop a prayer life but found, much to her frustration, that prayer remained difficult and unrewarding for her despite all her best efforts. In fact, prayer for her was boring and tiring, and often she just gave up trying.

Not long after her profession she fell ill with a mysterious sickness that would not respond to any treatment.[1] Her father took her to all the best doctors of the time but none could help, and Teresa's illness only worsened. Finally she fell into a coma so deep that people thought she was dead. The coma lasted four days and it's a good thing it didn't last a moment longer, as Teresa awoke to discover that a grave for her had been dug and was ready to receive her body. Following this her legs were paralyzed for the next three years.

Perhaps we would expect that this strange brush with death would have opened for Teresa the gates of prayer, that her spiritual life would deepen dramatically as a result of it. Apparently, however, the opposite happened. Although she had moments of deep prayer and even mystical experiences, these were fleeting, rare, and maddeningly unpredictable. For the most part she continued her lengthy period of, if not dryness, then a very average prayer life, although she wanted desperately to pray well, to lose herself in mental prayer. In fact, this was her great goal at this time, to rid herself of her worldliness and to turn constantly to God in prayer. She struggled with this for a long time and was greatly frustrated at the small improvements and frequent lapses she felt she was experiencing. Gradually she realized she was hampered in the development of her spiritual life by the very convent in which she lived. With one hundred forty nuns, it was much too large. The rules of enclosure had been so mitigated that the nuns regularly entertained friends and visitors in their parlor, and this was far too distracting. Teresa realized she was actually contributing to this problem herself, as her own vibrant personality was attracting visitors to the convent and interfering with the life she was trying so desperately and frustratingly to lead.

Teresa struggled on, striving to lead a life of vibrant mental prayer but never succeeding. That battle went on for two decades. She joined the Carmelites when she was twenty years old, and it was not until 1555, when she was forty, that the interior conversion she yearned for finally became a reality. This occurred at least partially from her encounter with the writings of Saint Augustine, whom we have already considered. In him she found someone she thought to be like herself. She saw in his difficulties in accepting the faith something similar to her difficulties in really living the religious life. She also was greatly helped by spiritual directors who came from outside the Carmelite order: Dominicans and Jesuits. Suddenly the spiritual life she had always wanted began to take root, and not in any average way. She began to experience intellectual visions, dramatic visions of Christ and the Cross. After so many years of dryness these seemed to penetrate her to her very soul, to open her up to prayer in deep and meaningful ways. The nun who couldn't pray was suddenly transformed into the nun whose prayer touched heaven.

But even here she had difficulty, as some people began to think that she was mad and others that her visions came from the devil. She experienced enormous turmoil and doubt over this until she was counseled by Saint Peter Alcantara, a Franciscan, who finally told her that her experiences were real and a great gift from God.

Once she attained this certitude her worldly ways became things of the past, and the deep prayer life she had yearned for was hers, never again to be lost. But all this convinced her that she could progress no further in her spiritual life until she was able to live a more austere form of the monastic life. She decided to found a Carmelite house which would adhere strictly to the primitive and very exacting form of the Carmelite rule. When she announced this project she was met with substantial opposition from both civil and religious authorities. In fact, she was denounced by almost every-body, including her own religious sisters. She was also threatened with the Inquisition (which was no small threat) and with legal prosecution. Most people would have run away in terror. Saint Teresa, however, just continued doing what she knew she should do until finally the local bishop came to her aid, and in 1562 the Convent of Saint Joseph came into existence. The life to be lived within its walls was radically different from the life lived by Teresa up to this point: extreme poverty was the rule, as was real hardship and a genuine enclosure. The nuns wore coarse brown habits and sandals rather than shoes; they ate no meat and depended for their food on their own work. Yet Teresa was insistent on joy in the life of her sisters. She knew that the life of the true Christian must be a life of joy, a life of constant transformation and growing ever closer to God. "May God protect me from gloomy saints," she is reputed to have commented, and this says much about the success of Teresa of Avila as a reformer.

The Convent of Saint Joseph was such a success that Saint Teresa began to found more such convents throughout Spain. She was indefatigable. Nothing could stop her including sweltering heat, terrible cold, the dangerous roads of Spain, or even the ire of other religious—which was blistering. She was regularly condemned by other convents and other religious orders. She was thought a dangerous troublemaker, a pawn of the devil. All this hatred came because she was trying to bring a genuine monasticism back into a world that had lost a sense of what the true religious life really was. Almost everyone seemed to be against her, but she prevailed, because she was doing God's work. Eventually she founded sixteen convents and her austere form of the religious life began to have an effect on other orders as well and to extend beyond the borders of Spain. During all this time, her prayer life continued to grow. She taught and wrote about prayer, transforming the lives of many and bringing a steady stream of new postulants to her convent doors.

In the later part of her life she encountered Saint John of the Cross, a fellow Carmelite and a fellow mystic. He may have lacked the practicality that made Saint Teresa so successful in whatever she undertook, but that didn't matter to her. She enlisted him to help her extend her reform to the Carmelite friars as well as the Carmelite nuns. Unsurprisingly, the two of them met with much opposition, but again they were successful. (We will see in the next section just what Saint John of the Cross had to endure.) The reforms of Saint Teresa began to penetrate deeply into the lives of many of the friars until they, like Saint Teresa's nuns, were recognized by the Church as a new Carmelite order, called the Discalced Carmelites.

The rest of Saint Teresa's life was spent in furthering her reform of monasticism and in writing. Her life was devoted to prayer and work, and she died exhausted at the age of sixty-seven after founding the sixteenth of her convents. Her writings today still provide extraordinary guidance in prayer in all its various forms and levels. Generations of Catholics and many, many saints have been taught to pray well by Saint Teresa of Avila, and we shall see later in this book that her autobiography was instrumental in bringing a young Jewish philosopher out of her atheism, into the Church, and eventually to sainthood.

Saint Teresa of Avila shows us that practicality and asceticism are not mutually exclusive. She shows us that God calls us in His own time to be saints—not on our schedules. She shows us—as does Saint Clare before her—that the austerities of monastic life and great joy go hand in hand. Saint Teresa of Avila is a saint of extraordinary depth who began life as a determined but worldly young woman. She is a saint who once despaired of being able to pray at all but whose prayer life eventually reached heights that few will ever know in this world. She is a saint whose life reminds us over and over again that all things are possible with God.

Saint Teresa of Avila, an Unexpected Guide

When I was a young man I had a thing for saints. Any saint could hold my interest, but I was particularly fascinated by cloistered religious. I'm not sure if it was the mystery of what lay behind those high monastery walls or whether it was simply an attraction to the more dramatic examples of religious life, but I was enthralled by any saint who had lived the enclosed life. I read about Trappists and Carthusians and Benedictines, and they were all very impressive. But when I came to Saint Teresa of Avila, I knew I had reached the summit. She seemed to me more an angel come to earth than a mere saint. I read her autobiography over and over again, trying to discover her secret, trying to find what made her so perfect. But the key always eluded me.

Eventually I did something I had dreamed about doing for years. I went to Avila and walked around the places that were important in Saint Teresa's life, particularly the Convent of the Incarnation, which is outside the city walls. This is where she went as a young woman. On that same trip I visited the much smaller convent in the city, which was dedicated to Saint Joseph. It was there that she began her great reform. On that trip something occurred to me. It came as a great realization and yet it was really a very ordinary and normal thought, and after it I began to see Saint Teresa of Avila differently and more clearly. I finally understood that she was a very human person. Everything in Avila spoke to me not of an otherworldly saint but of an earthy woman, a woman who despite her cloistered life was very much flesh and blood, a saint who shared in our human problems. At first I thought that my new way of looking at Saint Teresa would destroy my long-standing devotion to her. It was like finding out that your best friend isn't quite who you thought he was. I was no longer in awe of Saint Teresa; if that was gone what would remain?

As it turned out, quite a bit remained and some new things were discovered. Some years later I found myself in a situation that I had never anticipated. The religious community to which I belonged, the Capuchins, whom I loved and continue to love, had changed in ways that made it increasingly difficult for me to remain with them. As time went on I became aware that my beloved community and I were on progressively divergent paths, and that the time for me to leave was growing close. This caused me great heartache, and it caused great confusion and doubt, as well. The Capuchins had given me my home, my identity. To sever my ties with them would be like casting myself adrift. Was I in danger of becoming nothing more than a rudderless ship? I knew I was not totally alone, as there were a few others who might leave with me, but I felt very isolated. I was one frail human person putting behind me the life I had thought I would live until my earthly death, leaving behind me all the security that I had known.

It was then that my old friend Saint Teresa came back into my life in a way that she had not since that trip to Avila. She came as a mentor and a guide, for I realized that she had done in a much more dramatic and extensive way the very thing that I was contemplating. She had left the Carmelite convent of her youth, but she had not left Carmel. Instead she had brought Carmel with her in her heart and soul to a place where it could grow and flower again.

It was, at least in part, this hope that I drew from Saint Teresa of Avila that gave me the courage to do what I knew God was calling me to do. And so with Saint Teresa as a guide, eight heavy-hearted

Capuchins left our home for the uncertainty of forming a new religious community. We obviously have not accomplished anything like the reforms that Saint Teresa of Avila accomplished, and we never will. Yet in our hearts we carried our love of the Capuchin-Franciscan way of life with us, and we have tried to find a place for it to grow and flower again. With the constant help of Saint Teresa of Avila I believe we have succeeded, and for this reason she will forever be among the saints who are most important to me.

Saint Teresa continues to guide me. We are old friends and we talk a lot. I find myself composing little prayers to her from time to time: The following is one of the most recent. I thought I'd share it with you:

> Dearest Saint Teresa, my trusted companion and good friend for so many years, pray for me as I continue my struggle through this earthly life. You became my friend when I was young, but at this point in the journey, I am quite a bit older than you were when you went home to God. The pains and aches of life as well as its inevitable disappointments have become weighty burdens that can pull me down in ways that were not possible just a few years ago. Yet I am strengthened by the knowledge that you are with me. Your teachings have guided me; your life has given me a wonderful example to follow. You show me what the religious life can be. And you teach me how to pray. I thank you for your presence and your guidance. I ask you to continue to be with me, until that day when we shall meet in eternal life, that day when all burdens and struggles will finally be lifted and replaced by unending joy. Amen.

―――――――

Saint Teresa of Avila is one of the world's great guides to prayer, so it's only fitting that we should contemplate a prayer she herself composed.

O God of my soul, how we hasten to offend You and how You hasten even more to pardon us! What reason is there, Lord, for such deranged boldness? Could it be that we have already understood Your great mercy and have forgotten that Your justice is just?

The sorrows of death surround me. Oh, oh, oh, what a serious thing sin is, for it was enough to kill God with so many sorrows! And how surrounded You are by them, my God! Where can You go that they do not torment You? Everywhere mortals wound You.

O Christians, it's time to defend your King and to accompany Him in such great solitude. Few are the vassals remaining with Him, and great the multitude accompanying Lucifer. And what's worse is that these latter appear as His friends in public and sell Him in secret. He finds almost no one in whom to trust. O true Friend, how badly he pays You back who betrays You! O true Christians, help your God weep, for those compassionate tears are not only for Lazarus but for those who were not going to want to rise, even though His Majesty calls them. O my God, how You bear in mind the faults I have committed against You! May they now come to an end, Lord, may they come to an end, and those of everyone. Raise up these dead; may Your cries be so powerful that even though they do not beg life of You, You give it to them so that afterward, my God, they might come forth from the depth of their own delights.

Lazarus did not ask You to raise him up. You did it for a woman sinner; behold one here, my God, and a much greater one; let Your mercy shine. I, although miserable, ask life for those who do not want to ask it of You. You already know, my King, what torment it is for me to see them so forgetful of the great endless torments they will suffer, if they don't return to You.[2]

The strong emotion and awareness of sin in the previous passage is transformed by Saint Teresa into a deep awareness of God's overwhelming love in the following words:

As often as we think of Christ we should recall the love with which He bestowed on us so many favors and what great love God showed us in giving us a pledge like this of His love, for love begets love. Even if we are at the very beginning and are very wretched, let us strive to keep this divine love always before our eyes and to waken ourselves to love. If at some time the Lord should favor us by impressing this love on our hearts, all will become easy for us, and we shall carry out our tasks quickly and without much effort.[3]

10.

SAINT JOHN OF THE CROSS

"WE COME TO CARMEL TO SUFFER," Mother Marie de Gonzague said as Saint Thérèse of Lisieux lay dying of tuberculosis. These are strange and even offensive words to our modern ears, for so much of contemporary life involves the frantic avoidance of suffering. Our secular world sees suffering as wrong, as evil. Today we can find no meaning in it, and behind the meaninglessness of suffering our world glimpses what it believes to be the meaningless—the ultimate nothingness—of life itself. Therefore suffering must be avoided, denied, eradicated. It is an affront to the control we work so hard to exert over our own lives. We do not want to permit suffering to exist.

The saints, however, look at things differently—and far more deeply than our superficial culture can even imagine. We come now to Saint John of the Cross, a great saint who was no stranger to suffering. Indeed, suffering of one kind or another seemed to attend almost every part of his life. He knew the suffering of extreme poverty, of hunger, of illness, of hardship, of rejection, of imprisonment, and even of cruel physical abuse. Today we would expect a life so marked by suffering to culminate in despair—perhaps even in a denial of God. This, of course, is not what happened, because Saint John of the Cross found meaning in the suffering he endured, as he found ultimate meaning in the suffering Christ endured for us all. Saint John of the Cross was able to unite his suffering to that of Christ and thus find love and hope and even joy in suffering. The trials of his life enabled him to come closer and closer to God. They were for him gates of prayer and gates to God. Out of the sufferings of Saint John of the Cross came astonishing beauty: poems that have been called "among the most memorable in the Spanish language and perhaps in world literature."[1] Suffering led Saint John of the Cross to produce some of the greatest mystical writings of the Church, writings that continue to renew and deepen the faith of countless people.

So let's look at the life of this little friar, who was Saint Teresa's protégé and partner in renewal, and one of the greatest mystics the world has ever known.

THE MYSTICAL SAINT OF CARMEL

Saint John of the Cross was born Juan de Yepes y Alvarez in 1542 in the town of Fontiveros in Spain. The youngest of three sons born to Gonzalo de Yepes and Catalina Alvarez, John should have lived a life of comfort and prestige. His father came from a family of successful silk traders. They were wealthy and respected and could easily have given the boy anything he wanted in terms of worldly goods and education. Yet this saint grew up in abject poverty. John's mother, you see, came from a poor background, and the proud Yepes family simply could not accept her. Thus Gonzalo, his wife, and all their children were disowned and disinherited. Perhaps Gonzalo had imagined that his parents would eventually take him back, but this never happened and the little family descended into greater and greater poverty. When Juan was only two years old his father died, perhaps from the hardships he had endured in trying to support his family. Now they were plunged into absolutely desperate conditions. As if this were not difficult enough, the middle son of the family died only two years later.

Catalina tried her best to support herself and her sons as a silk weaver but barely brought in enough to keep the boys fed. Penniless, they moved from village to village throughout Castile in hopes of finding a better life, a life that always seemed to elude them. Finally they arrived at a town called Medina del Campo, where John was sent to a school for the poor. There he attempted to learn a trade but failed over and over again to acquire even the basic skills necessary to obtain employment. He also worked at an Augustinian convent as a sacristan, and perhaps it is here that his religious vocation began to grow.

Still only a boy, John was given a job that suited his low status in Spanish society. He worked in the hospital of Medina, caring for the poor and the dying, risking contagion and being exposed to all kinds of physical and mental suffering. This continued for several years, and at the same time he found he was able to attend a local Jesuit school. After four years of solid education, John was considered fit to join the Carmelite order, which had become his dream. Doing so changed his life completely. For the first time he was well treated. After he professed his solemn vows he was given access to the finest education available in Spain. No one had expected this poor boy to do very well in his studies, but he excelled. He did especially well in theology and scholastic philosophy, as well as all other areas of study needed for the priesthood, and he was ordained in 1567.

Returning to Medina del Campo to celebrate his first Mass, the young priest encountered a fellow Carmelite, a nun whose name he learned was Mother Teresa of Jesus. We know her as Saint Teresa of Avila. After this meeting the life of Saint John of the Cross was never to be the same again.

At this point Saint Teresa was fifty-two years old and John of the Cross was twenty-five. She was already well underway in her reform of the Carmelites and saw in this newly ordained priest a kindred soul, just the sort of person she needed to help her in her work. There was a problem, however: John, who was always given to silence and the interior life, was actually contemplating leaving the Carmelites, whom he thought too lax in their religious observance. His plan was to join the Carthusians, a very strict monastic community. Saint Teresa would not hear of it and lost no time in convincing John that his vocation lay with Carmel and that his efforts must be turned toward a reform of the order to restore its rigor and prayerfulness. It didn't take the charismatic Teresa very long to convince the young friar, and soon she had a perfect collaborator.

Up to this moment John of the Cross had been known in religious life as Juan de Santo Matia (John of Saint Matthias). However, when he stood at the threshold of giving himself over to the uncertainty of the reform that Saint Teresa was urging on him, he changed his name. It was from this point onward that he was known as "John of the Cross." It was as if he was saying that the efforts of reform would bring him to the Cross, itself, and as we shall see, he was right.

Just one year after his ordination John began a tiny Carmelite community which embraced a very severe form of monasticism. The small group of friars lived together in a little farmhouse and went about barefoot as a very visible symbol of their commitment to extreme poverty.[2]

As we saw, Saint Teresa's reforms stirred up the wrath of many people. Those of Saint John, however, seemed to produce even more vitriol. A very acrimonious rift began to grow between the Carmelites involved in the new reforms and those who wanted no change. In 1576 John of the Cross was actually kidnapped by fellow Carmelites who didn't want to give up their rather comfortable, worldly lives for a life of austerity and deep prayer. He was imprisoned in a tiny cell with only one small window. The cell was cold and damp in the winter and stifling in the summer. Yet he was forced to spend all his time in it except for a few hours each week when he was taken out for the sole purpose of being beaten by his fellow religious. They demanded that he repudiate his reforms, but he would not. His health failing, he stood firm for nearly nine intolerable months, at which point he finally managed to escape.

Despite the horrors that he had endured, John of the Cross actually experienced great beauty during his time of imprisonment. His soul had been comforted by Christ, and in that cell his prayer life had flourished as never before. During this terrible time he also wrote some of the most beautiful and mystical poetry that the world has ever seen. This was a transforming moment for him. Despite the evil that had been done to him by those who claimed to be his brothers, the good that he had experienced in the depths of his soul won out. From this point onward John of the Cross's life was devoted to showing to others the greatness of God's love.

Saint John of the Cross spent most of the rest of his life in furthering the reforms that Saint Teresa had initiated. Although his health was frail he founded monasteries throughout Spain. After the death of Saint Teresa in 1582 he served for a time as vicar provincial of the Carmelites in Andalusia, but even then turmoil and suffering were never far away. There arose serious conflicts within the order, resulting in different factions. Saint John gave his support to the one he thought best, but it was the others who gained power. As a result of this he was deprived of any position of power within the order and sent to one of the poorest of the monasteries to live in virtual seclusion. In other words he was betrayed and abandoned by the very order he had suffered so much to found.

Saint John of the Cross died on December 14, 1591. At the very end of his life even those who had mistreated him had to recognize his holiness, as has every generation since.

In Saint John of the Cross we have a saint who actually prayed "to suffer and be despised." And it certainly seems that his prayer was answered. Yet despite his many sufferings we have a saint who lived an interior life of great—almost indescribable—

joy. He left behind works that rank with the greatest mystical literature of the Church and poems that express a love of God so profound and exultant that they are unmatched. Saint John of the Cross shows us what the world denies, that our life is truly with God and not to be found among the cares of this world. He shows us that while we are suffering terribly in this world we may still be united in profound and lasting joy with Christ. Saint John of the Cross is a saint who shows very clearly the true depths of the life God has given us.

THE SPIRITUAL ALCHEMY OF
SAINT JOHN OF THE CROSS

Do you remember hearing about the alchemists of the Middle Ages? Alchemists were people who believed that there was a way to turn lead into gold. Some of them apparently labored their entire lives to find the process that would accomplish this and thus become rich. Of course the process was never found, since it did not exist. It is simply not possible to transmute one element into another. Eventually the idea of alchemy simply faded away to be replaced by more reasonable pastimes.

Are you surprised that I'm talking about alchemy when you expected me to be talking about Saint John of the Cross? I admit that at first glance there doesn't seem to be any connection. Yet if we look a little more closely I believe we shall see that there is. You see, Saint John of the Cross actually did find a way to turn lead into gold. Now, I certainly mean this in a symbolic rather than literal sense, but a real one nonetheless. Here was a man who lived a difficult life, who was confronted by troubles and sufferings nearly around every corner. Most of us would rebel, give up, even curse God if we lived the life of John of the Cross. But he not only accepted the sufferings he was given; he used them in a truly glorious way. He transformed them—transmuted them like lead into gold—into a great mystical experience of God, into a closeness to God that is almost unmatched in the history of the Church. And from this experience sprang writings that amaze and challenge us to this day, as well as lyric poetry that is haunting and extraordinarily beautiful, poetry that speaks eloquently of the great love of God for man. This was a love that Saint John of the Cross experienced powerfully in his interior life, although on the surface he lived a life that many people today would see as all but devoid of God's love.

There are some famous but mysterious words of Saint Paul from the Letter to the Colossians that always come into my mind when I contemplate Saint John of the Cross: "Now I rejoice in my sufferings for your sake, and in my flesh I complete what is lacking in Christ's afflictions for the sake of his body, that is the church" (Col 1:24). Many people today can make no sense of these words, but they certainly must have had great meaning for Saint John of the Cross, so much meaning that he was able to transmute these words into reality. By completely uniting his sufferings with those of Christ he was able to live his difficult life here on earth with a constant awareness of the reality and closeness of the Kingdom of God. In a way we can say that he inhabited two worlds at once.

I am no Saint John of the Cross, and I have to say that there are times when the suffering that attends every human life gets me down. When I was hit by a car some years ago I was left with certain disabilities that were unknown to me before that event. Walking up a flight of stairs, something that I always did without a thought, now is an ordeal. Many of the normal things of life have become difficult and aggravating. I have become aware that I am easily frustrated. There are days when I wish I were in purgatory rather than here on earth.

It is during these times that I become especially aware of Saint John of the Cross. I try to look to him as a model. He teaches me over and over again how to deal with difficulties that cannot be overcome, that are simply part of the facts of our lives. He teaches me that although the pain of life may not disappear it can be used to turn closer and closer to Christ, who endured so much pain for us all.

I sometimes reread the poetry of Saint John of the Cross, and I often turn to his mystical writings. Each time, I am overawed to realize that such beauty and faith could coexist with so much suffering. Each time I am renewed as I watch Saint John of the Cross turn the lead of suffering into the gold of hope, and faith, and a beauty that is so intense that it can only have come from a deep experience of the Holy Trinity. I myself am no alchemist, and I never will be one. For that I turn to Saint John of the Cross, and I know he will never fail to turn the lead in my life to gold.

———

The following words are from a work called The Spiritual Canticle. *In it Saint John expounds on the unfathomable riches and mysteries of Christ that await the soul determined to seek Him above all things.*

There is much to fathom in Christ, for He is like an abundant mine with many recesses of treasures, so that however deep men go they never reach the end or bottom, but rather in every recess find new veins with new riches everywhere. On this account St. Paul said of Christ: *In Christ dwell hidden all treasures and wisdom* (Col 2:3). The soul cannot enter these caverns or reach these treasures if, as we said, she does not first pass over to the divine wisdom through the straits of exterior and interior suffering. For one cannot reach in this life what is attainable of these mysteries of Christ without having suffered much, and without having received numerous intellectual and sensible favors from God, and without having undergone much spiritual activity; for all these favors are inferior to the wisdom of the mysteries of Christ in that they serve as preparations for coming to this wisdom. When Moses asked God to reveal His glory, God told Moses that he would be unable to receive such a revelation in this life, but that he would be shown all good, that is, all the good revealable in this life. So God put Moses in the cavern of the rock, which is Christ, as we said, and showed His back to him, which was to impart knowledge of the mysteries of the humanity of Christ.

The soul, then, longs earnestly to enter these caverns of Christ in order to be absorbed, transformed, and wholly inebriated in the love of the wisdom of these mysteries, and hide herself in the bosom of the Beloved.[3]

11.

Saint Peter Canisius

I RECENTLY PASSED THE FIFTY-SECOND anniversary of my priestly ordination, which is something that seems impossible to me, but it is true nonetheless. It's hard to imagine how much has happened over those many years, and sometimes it's also hard to admit that the world in which we live seems to have gone so far downhill during that time. It is sad to say, but that seems especially true as we look at the Church. The Church in which I was ordained in 1959 appeared very different from the Church of 2011. In those far-off years it seemed that the Church was an impregnable fortress. She was bursting at the seams with people, most of whom seemed reasonably devout. Her school system was the envy of every other religious body and produced articulate students who knew the faith. Her colleges and universities were outstanding and truly Catholic. Her religious communities were numerous and seemed vibrant.

That was the Church of my youth. The Church of my later years appears very different. So many of her institutions are diminished or even on the verge of collapse that there is no point in trying even to list them here. It sometimes seems as if we stand among ruins, as if the Church in the West is but a remnant of what it once was.

The preceding words may sound as if I'm discouraged, as if I've given up hope, but that's far from the truth. I am, in fact, quite encouraged, for there are many signs of hope and renewal—even if we sometimes have to search a little to find them. Often these signs of hope are small and as yet not very powerful, but they are becoming more numerous and slowly gaining momentum. I'm looking forward to watching their progress, which I intend to do mostly from a good seat in purgatory.

What has all this to do with Saint Peter Canisius? Plenty. If we think we have it bad today, we don't know what "bad" really is, and if there's anyone who could tell us what a Church in disaster mode looks like it's this saint. Saint Peter Canisius faced a Church that was disintegrating before his very eyes. He spent most of this priestly ministry in Germany at a time when people were deserting Catholicism in droves for the new Protestant religious bodies, especially Lutheranism. Yet Peter Canisius was not discouraged. He felt armed with the truth and supported by the Holy Spirit. And he accomplished wonders in defending the Church from her attackers and bringing back many who had strayed. It has been said that Catholicism in German lands survived because of Saint Peter Canisius. So let's take at look at this astonishing Counter-Reformation saint, who stood in the ruins of the Church and, far from losing hope, simply set to work rebuilding those ruins— practically by himself.

The Saint Who Turned the Tide of the Reformation

In 1517 Martin Luther published his famous *Ninety-Five Theses on the Power and Efficacy of Indulgences,* thus providing the spark that would ignite the Protestant Reformation. The resulting split in Western Christianity was tragic and still remains unhealed today. Four years later in the town of Nijmegen, which is in present-day Holland, a boy named Petrus (or Peter) Canisius was born to devout Catholic parents. His father, Jacob, was a wealthy burgomaster; his mother died when Peter was still a baby. As Peter grew, it became apparent that he was of unusual intelligence, and his proud father wanted him to have the best education available. Accordingly the boy was sent to the University of Cologne, where he studied law, theology, and the arts. While there he was attracted to a nearby Carthusian monastery and found in the austere life of the monks a great source of inspiration and a strong support for his faith. He also studied at the University of Louvain for a short period before receiving the degree of Master of Arts at Cologne. During his university career Peter became acquainted with some Catholics who had come to both Cologne and Louvain in search of a place where they could practice their Catholic faith without fear of persecution, for their lands of origin had become staunchly Protestant. This situation disturbed the young man greatly.

Jacob Canisius looked forward to the day when his son would take a wife and give him the grandchildren he desired, so this doting father was probably rather disturbed to discover that at the age of eighteen his son—dreaming of giving his life to God in some way—had already taken the rather dramatic step of formally pledging himself to a life of celibacy.

Peter considered the Carthusians, who had meant so much to him. He was deeply attracted to them but realized that the life of a monk was not the life to which God was calling him. In 1543 he made a visit to one of Saint Ignatius Loyola's early followers, Peter Faber, and was introduced by him to the Ignatian spiritual exercises, which Peter found to be powerful aids in deepening his spiritual life. At that time the Society of Jesus was only three years old and faced an uncertain future, but Peter Canisius immediately knew he had found the right home, the home that God had prepared for him. He applied for admittance and was quickly accepted, becoming the first Dutchman to join the new order.

Things tended to move quickly in the life of Peter Canisius. He was ordained to the priesthood in June 1546 and the very next year found himself at the Council of Trent[1] as a minor theologian. Later he was brought to Rome by Saint Ignatius where, after several months, he made his final profession as a Jesuit; and then received a doctorate in theology from the University of Bologna. In 1548 he taught in Sicily, but while he was there the Duke of Bavaria petitioned the Pope to send educators to Bavaria to combat the growing Protestant influence. Peter Canisius, who was among the first to be sent, discovered on his arrival that the University of Ingolstadt had fallen into Protestant hands. He immediately set about to correct this and succeeded so well that in 1550 he found himself the rector of the university. Just two years later he was on the move again, this time sent by Saint Ignatius to Vienna, which was not a place a fainthearted Catholic would want to visit at that time.

Why is that? I think I'll let my good friend, the wonderful Jesuit Father John Hardon, tell you. Father Hardon once delivered an excellent talk on Saint Peter Canisius, and I'm using a transcription of that as one of my sources in writing this piece. These are his words about the religious situation in Vienna when Peter Canisius arrived in the Austrian capital: "[M]any of the parishes were without priests; the large archdiocese of Vienna had not had one ordination in twenty years; monasteries were abandoned; religious were jeered in the streets; ninety percent of the Catholics gave up their faith; ten percent of the Catholics barely practiced their faith; more than once Peter Canisius preached to empty churches."[2] And we think we've got it bad?

What did Peter Canisius do? Just about everything. Again, I'll let Father Hardon tell you part of it: "He won the people over by his practice of charity, especially to the sick and the plague stricken."[3] (We must never underestimate this. The power of charity and kindness is of incalculable value in making Christ known to people. A Christian who is indifferent to the needs of others can hardly be called a Christian at all.) Peter Canisius also taught theology at the university, allowing true Catholic doctrine to be known clearly and probably for the first time in a great while. He preached tirelessly to almost anyone who would listen. Apparently one of those who would listen was King Ferdinand I, and it was a good thing that he did, for a real problem was brewing right in the palace. The king's eldest son, Crown Prince Maximilian, had become entranced by the new Protestant approach to things and had secured an appointment as Preacher to the Royal Court for a man named Phauser, who had been ordained a Catholic priest but who was married and was preaching Lutheran doctrine. It looked as if the crown prince was at the point of declaring himself a Protestant. If he did so and then ascended to the throne, Peter Canisius knew that Austria would be lost to the Church, possibly forever. Although a naturally kind man, he spoke in the bluntest of terms to both the king and the crown prince, and he actually convinced King Ferdinand to disinherit his son if the son should convert. That ended the problem.

For his astonishing work of bringing Austria, both royalty and common people, back into the Church's fold, the Pope attempted to appoint Peter Canisius Archbishop of Vienna, but since Jesuits are prevented by vow from becoming bishops, Peter became instead "Administrator of the Bishopric of Vienna" for one year.

Soon he was traveling again, opening Jesuit colleges in Ingolstadt and in Prague. At almost the same time he was named the first Jesuit provincial superior of Upper Germany. He took part in a meeting between Catholics and Protestants called the Colloquy of Worms, at which Philip Melanchthon (the most important figure in the formation of Lutheranism after Luther himself and a highly capable theologian) was also present. At this meeting Peter Canisius apparently was able to point out to his Protestant opponents certain inconsistencies and problems in the doctrines they were espousing, and it is said that by the time the colloquy ended the Protestant attendees were rather in disarray.

Understanding that in order for the Faith to be lived it must first be taught, Peter Canisius did whatever he could to establish sound Catholic educational institutions. In 1559 he opened a college in Munich and was responsible for the establishment of Catholic schools throughout the German-speaking world. He also returned to the Council of Trent, this time as a prominent theologian, and when the council was finally over, it became his task to bring its decrees to the German bishops—not an easy job, and one that took him through Protestant territories that were so anti-Catholic that his very life was in danger. Despite this Peter Canisisus realized that peace between Christian factions was a vital goal and he worked to establish and support treaties between Catholics and Protestants. Through his efforts in this area much bloodshed was probably averted.

Even as he aged Peter Canisius remained tireless. He moved from Augsburg, to Innsbruck, to Ratisbon, and to many other places, all with one purpose: to reestablish the Church where she had disappeared and to keep Catholics from becoming Protestant. In the process of all this, his example attracted many young men to the Jesuit order. By 1580 the Jesuits were a powerful force throughout German-speaking lands, primarily due to this one man.

During the last decade and a half of Peter Canisius's life, he finally stopped his wandering. He came to Freiburg and began yet another school. It evolved into a great Jesuit center and a bastion of Catholicism that lasted for centuries. He died in 1597 at the age of seventy-six. When he began his work it seemed as if all German speaking lands would inevitably become Lutheran. At his death almost all of southern Germany was solidly Catholic, and this can be attributed directly to him.

In Saint Peter Canisius we have a saint to whom we should look often. Here was a man who stood in the ruins of the Church, a man who began his career at a time when most people believed the Catholic Church was doomed in northern Europe. He was one lone man who accepted God's call to do the impossible, and yet he succeeded brilliantly because he knew he was never really alone, that he was working as God's instrument and was doing God's will.

Ruins and Visions:
What Peter Canisius Has Shown Me

Most of the saints I have chosen to write about in this book have been with me in one way or another for much of my life. Peter Canisius is different. I have found him only relatively recently. I knew about him, of course, and I even admired him. Yet I never really developed a devotion to this great Jesuit saint until the last few years.

I believe this illustrates something important about our relationship with the saints. Each saint is different, a unique and unrepeatable aspect of God's creation. Thus it is probable that we will be immediately attracted to certain saints and perhaps not to others. Some of them will speak deeply to our lives, to our personal situations, while others may not; and that's the way it must be. It is also likely that different saints will mean different things to us at various times in our lives. Our relationship with certain saints does not end as we go from one stage to another in our journey to God, but some saints who seemed very important to us in our youth may recede somewhat, while others we may not even have thought about when we were young come increasingly to prominence as we age.

So it has been for Saint Peter Canisius and me. In recent years I have come to find him a great help. I see personal meaning in his life that I did not see when I was a young friar. In Peter Canisius I have found a saint who was at the very center of European history. He was a leader of the Church who refused to be daunted by the seemingly irresistible spread of Protestantism in the German-speaking lands of Europe. Peter Canisius did all that was in his power to defend the Church that he loved at a time and in a place where it seemed that the Church was doomed—and, with the help of the Holy Spirit, Peter Canisius triumphed. It was through this saint that God breathed new life into a Church which appeared to be at the point of death.

The Church is again in a time of difficulty and turmoil. She is often mocked and disregarded. She is frequently attacked outright. It seems at times as if Catholicism and even Christianity in general are fatally wounded in the Western world. Many already say we inhabit a "post-Christian" world, and the signs of this are everywhere. Recently same-sex marriage has been declared legal in my home state of New York. How utterly un-Christian is a view of marriage that sees nothing wrong in redefining it in this way? How utterly secular, how totally free of any remnant of Christian thinking is an understanding of marriage that includes nothing more than a contract and a list of rights and privileges granted by the state? Can we even imagine a more impoverished and materialistic view of marriage? It sometimes seems that the awareness of God is simply vanishing from our world, evaporating like water in the summer sun.

When we are tempted to become discouraged about such things, it is Saint Peter Canisius to whom we should turn. He would not be daunted. He would simply redouble his efforts to defend the Church in her time of great need. Through his example and with the help of his prayers, I have often found the strength to do whatever is in my own limited power to defend and support the Church that I have loved for my entire life. In Peter Canisius I have found a holy life that proclaims to all who have ears to listen that the Church can never be fatally wounded, that faith and courage and the will to preach the Gospel of Christ are all that's really needed to breathe new life into a Church that only seems at times to be moribund. "Be not afraid," said the great Pope John Paul II so often and to so many people that these words could have been his official motto. Those words could have been the motto of Saint Peter Canisius, as well. In Peter Canisius I have found a saint who truly lived by those words. And in my newfound relationship with this wonderful saint I have come to see that these are the words we all must learn to live by as we follow Saint Peter Canisius's example and rebuild our beloved Church.

A Contemporary German Catholic's Words of Thanks to Saint Peter Canisius

We depart a little from our usual pattern here. Instead of including a few paragraphs of the writings of Saint Peter Canisius, I thought it might be a good idea to look at what one of his spiritual descendants had to say about him. Pope Benedict XVI spoke about Peter Canisius during an audience given in February 2011. As a German, the Pope is well aware that his own family's ties to the Church may not have existed if not for this saint.

I believe that the Pope has much to say in the following excerpt, not only about Peter Canisius but about many other important things, as well.

———

Characteristic of St. Canisius' spirituality was a profound personal friendship with Jesus. For example, on Sept. 4, 1549, he wrote in his diary, speaking with the Lord: "In the end, as if you opened to me the heart of the Most Sacred Body, which it seemed to me I saw before me, you commanded me to drink from that source, inviting me, so to speak, to attain the waters of my salvation from your founts, O my Savior." And then he saw that the Savior gave him a garment with three parts that were called peace, love and perseverance. And with this garment made up of peace, love and perseverance, Canisius carried out his work of renewal of Catholicism. His friendship with Jesus—which is the center of his personality—nourished by love of the Bible, by love of the Sacrament, by love of the Fathers, this friendship was clearly united to the awareness of being a continuer of the mission of the Apostles in the Church. And this reminds us that every genuine evangelizer is always a united instrument with Jesus and the Church and, because of this, fruitful.

St. Peter Canisius was formed in his friendship with Jesus in the spiritual environment of the Carthusian monastery of Cologne, in which he was in close contact with two Carthusian mystics: Johann Lansperger, Latinized into Lanspergius, and Nicholas van Hesche, Latinized into Eschius. Subsequently he deepened the experience of that friendship, *familiaritas stupenda nimis*, with the contemplation of the mysteries of Jesus' life, which form a large part of St. Ignatius' spiritual exercises. His intense devotion to the Lord's Heart, which culminated in consecration to the apostolic ministry in the Vatican Basilica, has its foundation here.

Rooted in the Christocentric spirituality of St. Peter Canisius is a profound conviction: There is no soul solicitous of its own perfection that does not practice mental prayer every day, an ordinary means that permits the disciple of Jesus to live in intimacy with the divine Master. Because of this, in the writings destined to the spiritual education of the people, our saint insists on the importance of the liturgy with his comments on the Gospels, on feasts, on the rite of the holy Mass and on the sacraments but, at the same time, he is careful to show to the faithful the need and the beauty of personal daily prayer, which should support and permeate participation in the public worship of the Church.[4]

12.

SAINT MARTIN DE PORRES

I WAS FOR MANY YEARS diocesan postulator for the Cause of Canonization of my dear friend Cardinal Terence Cooke. I knew Cardinal Cooke well and long before his death understood him to be a man of unusual holiness, someone I could really believe was a living saint. Yet Cardinal Cooke appeared in many ways to be very ordinary. He was the sort who could disappear into a crowd. You had to look closely to see his holiness, and since most people never look closely at anything, they often missed it. To my mind the saintliness of Cardinal Cooke was most clearly seen in his kindness, which was ever-present and absolutely unfailing. Cardinal Cooke was kind to everyone—to every creature—and that's not an easy thing to be. Kindness is an often overlooked element of the Christian life. As a virtue it seems run-of-the-mill, earthbound. There is nothing dramatic in kindness (as there was nothing dramatic about Cardinal Cooke), nothing mystical. Yet kindness should be at the very heart of the Christian life. I am sad to say that all too often it isn't.

The saint we are considering in this chapter reminds me of Cardinal Cooke. Saint Martin de Porres is a saint of kindness. Like Cardinal Cooke, Martin de Porres exhibited kindness to everyone and every creature he ever met. In Saint Paul's Second Letter to the Corinthians we read: "Therefore, if any one is in

Christ, he is a new creation; the old has passed away, behold, the new has come" (2 Cor 5:17). Isn't it possible that one of the many things Saint Paul may be saying here as he speaks of a "new creation" is that the life of the true Christian is a life that has put aside old hatreds, animosities, and selfishness, that sees the image of God in every person and the holiness inherent in all God's creatures? Since the first moment human beings walked the face of the earth we have had an overabundance of unkindness and indifference toward others. It has always been the natural way of things, and for most people it remains that. I believe that we take a step toward becoming a "new creation" when we begin to treat all creatures with the love and kindness with which God treats us, with the love and kindness that Jesus showed us during his earthly life. So maybe kindness is not so run-of-the-mill after all but a real key to the Christian life.

Let us look at the life of Saint Martin de Porres, an apostle of kindness, as we resolve to become the "new creation" we are meant to be.

THE SAINT WHO LOVED EVERY LIVING CREATURE

The beginnings of Martin de Porres's life were, to put it mildly, inauspicious. He was born on December 9, 1579, in Lima, the capital city of Peru. His father was a Spanish nobleman named Don Juan de Porres, and his mother was named Aña Velasquez; she was black and a freed slave who came originally from Panama. Martin's parents never married, although they produced another child, a daughter named Juana, who was born about three years later. As often happened in such circumstances, Martin's father abandoned the family, leaving them virtually penniless. Aña was a loving mother and did her best to support her children, but she simply could not do it alone, and the two children were reared in a type of poverty that we can hardly imagine.

When Martin was still only a boy he had what some might call an incredibly lucky break and others might call a small miracle:

he was given the opportunity to go to school. This he did for two years and at that point was apprenticed to a barber-surgeon, where he learned the medical arts, such as they were at that time. Naturally compassionate and unfailingly kind, Martin took to this work very readily. In fact, he found real joy in caring for others, and this he did with the greatest of concern. At the same time that he was devoting his life to the corporal works of mercy, Martin was developing a deep spiritual life. He was spending almost all of his free time in prayer. His love of God and the Blessed Mother (to whom he was especially devoted) was steadily growing, and so was his love of others. The kindness that he showed to those for whom he cared was so consistent and warm that the people around Martin were amazed.

At the age of fifteen, Martin presented himself at the local Dominican priory and asked to become a servant there. Sadly, because of his racial background, he was not regarded as eligible to enter the order. Even if he were, however, considering Martin's deep humility, it is somewhat doubtful that he would even have asked. It wasn't long before this new servant boy showed himself to be different from others. His deep faith and holy way of life could not be ignored, and it wasn't long before he became known in the priory as "the saint with the broom." This led to his being permitted to become a Dominican tertiary, and some years later he was admitted as a lay brother to the Order of Preachers. Martin's holy presence made them see for the first time the injustice of excluding people who were not of European descent. That's an accomplishment.

Amazingly Martin de Porres was made almoner of the Dominican community in Lima. In other words it was his job to obtain (usually by begging) the funds necessary for the friars to live and to carry on their work with the people of Lima. Although the humble Martin would never ask for anything for himself, he was astonishingly successful in this new position, and it is said that he was able to obtain the equivalent of two thousand dollars from the rich of the city each week.

Despite his success as an almoner, Martin found his true calling in the priory's infirmary. It was there that he spent most of his time, caring for the sick with great tenderness. He also cared for those outside the order, lay people who had no one else. He eventually established an orphanage and a hospital for the children of the poor. Miraculous cures were not rare among those cared for by this little Dominican brother, and his fame as a living saint began to spread throughout South America. One day he encountered an elderly beggar on the streets of Lima. The man was absolutely exhausted. He was also filthy, dressed in a few rags, and had oozing sores all over his body. Most of us would have recoiled at the sight—and probably the smell—of such a person. Martin de Porres, however, was able to see beyond the dirt and the grime. He knew that the image of God burned brightly in this pathetic man despite his outward appearance. Without a second thought, Brother Martin brought the man to his own room and let him sleep in his bed. When another brother criticized him for this, Brother Martin is said to have gently responded: "Compassion, my dear Brother, is preferable to cleanliness."

As I said earlier, kindness marked every moment of Martin de Porres's life, and it was a kindness that extended not just to people but to every living creature he encountered. Often we have difficulty seeing animals as creatures of God in their own right. We frequently think of them almost as objects for our use or even our amusement. This is spiritual blindness, and it can at times become a sinful and willful blindness, resulting in cruelty and abuse. Martin, however, saw every living being as created by the love of God, and he extended his own love to every living being he met—including even vermin. Martin de Porres could never ignore a sick or frightened animal, just as he could never ignore a person in need. In a time long before veterinary medicine had come into existence, he established a hospital for animals at his sister's home. There he lovingly administered to them the same remedies he used on people, and with much success. It is said that he even performed surgeries on these animals when needed. Martin's love of all God's creatures was so great that he could never bring himself to eat meat or even fish at all, and so spent most of his life as a vegetarian.

There are countless stories about this humble yet great saint, and all of them involve his kindness. There are stories of him risking his life to help his fellow Dominicans during a time of plague; there are stories of him distributing all of the money that had been given to him by the rich to the poor and indigent; there are stories of him helping the poorest of the poor in ways we can hardly imagine. Many of these stories have surely become embellished over time. Yet each one of them holds a kernel of truth: that in his great kindness and compassion to all God's creatures—both human and animal—Saint Martin of Porres consistently acted in a Christlike way throughout his life

Martin de Porres died on November 3, 1639, when he was only a month short of his sixtieth birthday. Six decades earlier he had come into this world as an illegitimate, mixed-race boy of no value. Yet at the time of his death he was known to all and loved by all. For nearly sixty years he did one thing consistently that some people never do at all. He showed the importance of kindness in the Christian life. He stands with Saint Francis and Blessed Mother Teresa of Calcutta—and my good friend Terry Cooke—in showing us what true mercy and compassion really are, what true saintliness can be—what it really means to be a "new creation."

From Symbol to Saint, My Evolving Friendship with Martin de Porres

When I was growing up, Saint Martin de Porres was becoming extremely popular with Catholics in the eastern United States. In fact, he was actually becoming a symbol for us. Segregation was at last at the point of being overcome in many parts of this country, and we were becoming more friendly with people of other races. We were actually beginning to see them as made in the image of God, just as we were. And if you're too young to remember those days, take it from me, this was something of a miracle. The Civil Rights movement was gathering steam at that time, and I was very much part of it, even as a young boy. It was during those days, a time when real change for the better seemed to be in the air, that I, too, discovered this saint, who was half European and half African. I liked him. I often gave out little blessed statues of Saint Martin, and I remember how eagerly people received them and how much they liked this saint with his Dominican habit and dark skin.

There was much good in the devotion that people had to Saint Martin de Porres back then, but there was a subtle down side, as well. As I said, we had made of Saint Martin a symbol of racial equality. As I look back at those days I realize that this saint, like any saint or any ordinary person, is diminished by being made into a symbol. It robs him of his humanness; it obscures the real value of an individual life, a life that is unrepeatable and unique.

As I said at the beginning of this chapter, there is something in Martin de Porres that reminds me of Cardinal Terence Cooke. Now, no two people could be less alike on the surface than a poor Peruvian Dominican lay brother and an Irish-American Archbishop of New York. But they were similar nonetheless in their understanding of Christianity, which was simple and direct—and very profound. Both of them knew in the very depths of their souls that each of God's living creations had great value. This is something that should be very basic to the Christian life but often is not. Saint Martin de Porres and Cardinal Cooke would go to great lengths to help and protect others. Neither of them would ever dream of slighting another person. Each of them felt real pain when they saw another person being injured in any way.

We live in a world that is so blinded by sin that casual cruelties are the norm and indifference to the pain of others is common. The infliction of little injuries on those we don't like is almost a pastime. When we are tempted to join the world in acting this way, instead we can turn to Saint Martin de Porres. For years I have tried to do so myself. I have often asked him to help me put aside those little moments of anger, those small temptations to belittle someone else that come to us all so regularly. He has helped me greatly and he continues to do so. And after all these years I still need this help.

Over time I have developed a devotion to Martin de Porres that has little to do with racial equality. We have come a long way toward achieving that in this country, although much work remains to be done, and we don't really need him as a symbol of that any longer. For me Martin de Porres's racial background has become incidental. I see him now as a very great saint and a very humble one. When I look at this simple lay brother whose spiritual life was probably far more vibrant than those of his religious superiors, I am always reminded that God chooses the most unlikely candidates for real holiness. So often the great saints would go unnoticed if we passed them on the street; so often their holiness flows out of something as ordinary as kindness. I urge everyone reading this book to pray to Martin de Porres, to meditate on his life and his gentleness, and to learn from him. This is important, for in saints like Martin de Porres we see what it is to take the very ordinary things of our lives and transform them into something extraordinary, something holy. In saints like Martin de Porres we really see what God wants from our lives.

———

Saint Martin de Porres did not leave us much in the way of writings, so we will go instead to something written about him. The following is an excerpt from a homily preached by Blessed John XXIII on the occasion of the canonization of Martin de Porres.

The example of Martin's life is ample evidence that we can strive for holiness and salvation as Christ Jesus has shown us: first, by loving God "with all your heart, with all your soul, and with all your mind; and second, by loving your neighbor as yourself."

When Martin had come to realize that Christ Jesus "suffered for us and that he carried our sins on his body to the cross," he would meditate with remarkable ardor and affection about Christ on the cross. Whenever he would contemplate Christ's terrible torture he would be reduced to tears. He had an exceptional love for the great sacrament of the Eucharist and often spent long hours in prayer before the Blessed Sacrament. His desire was to receive the sacrament in Communion as often as he could.

Saint Martin, always obedient and inspired by his divine teacher, dealt with his brothers with that profound love which comes from pure faith and humility of spirit. He loved men because he honestly looked on them as God's children and as his own brothers and sisters. Such was his humility that he loved them even more than himself, and considered them to be better and more righteous than he was.

He did not blame others for their shortcomings. Certain that he deserved more severe punishment for his sins than others did, he would overlook their worst offenses. He was tireless in his efforts to reform the criminal, and he would sit up with the sick to bring them comfort. For the poor he would provide food, clothing, and medicine. He did all he could to care for poor farmhands, blacks, and mulattoes who were looked down upon as slaves, the dregs of society in their time. Common people responded by calling him, "Martin the charitable."[1]

13

Saint Benedict Joseph Labré

Catholics have lots of names. We receive at least one and usually two at our baptism. We generally acquire another at our confirmation, and if we enter religious life we're apt to end up with yet another name or two. Like most Catholics I have an ample assortment of names, most of which we're not going to go into here. However, the time has come for us to discuss the name I chose when I made my first vows as a Capuchin back in 1951. Although most people simply call me Father Benedict, my full name is Father Benedict Joseph, and I picked that name to honor a saint who fascinated me then and continues to fascinate me today. Yes, I said *a* saint, not two. Perhaps you thought that the name Benedict Joseph was in honor of Saint Benedict of Nursia and Saint Joseph, the foster father of our Lord. That's a very reasonable guess—and a very Catholic one—but despite my devotion to both those great saints, I chose as my patron a saint who is far less known, a saint who was a misfit in his own time and would probably be even more so in ours.

Saint Benedict Joseph Labré was, in the world's terms, both a failure and a rather strange character. He wanted desperately to live the monastic life but was rejected by every monastery to which he tried to gain entrance. He came from a well-to-do bourgeois background, yet wandered the highways and byways of Europe for years living a life of poverty so extreme that even Saint Francis would have approved of it. He was often considered a fool and was regularly ridiculed. In fact, he may have been mentally ill. At the age of thirty-five he died a homeless beggar on the streets of Rome. Yet at his death crowds began to gather in the very streets in which Benedict Joseph Labré spent his last days, crowds that chanted over and over again *"È morto il santo!"* (The saint is dead!).

So I am very excited to share with you the life and unusual holiness of this uncommon saint, whose name I have tried to bear worthily for over half a century.

The Vagabond Saint

Benedict Joseph Labré entered this life on March 26, 1783, in the town of Amettes, in the northeastern part of France, not far from what is today the border with Belgium. He was brought up in a very ordinary bourgeois family. The son of a shopkeeper, Benedict had fourteen siblings, which sounds astounding to us today, but large families of that size were not uncommon throughout Europe at that time. The future saint received his early education in the local parish school. During that period in France this was the primary source of learning for most children, although that would change drastically and disastrously in the days of the French Revolution.

From his very early youth Benedict was different from other children. He displayed a real seriousness that is unusual for a boy of his age. He was also very devout and evidenced a real love of solitude and prayer. Thinking their eldest son was surely made for a religious vocation, his parents sent him to live and study with the boy's uncle, who was the parish priest of the town of Erin. His four-year period there was one during which his desire for solitude and prayer grew stronger and stronger. He also displayed great charity and compassion toward others, something that would mark the rest of Benedict Joseph's life. He taught small children and did all that was within his power to help the sick. When he was still in his early teens, plague struck the area in which he lived. Fear of contagion was great, and many people ignored or even abandoned the afflicted; yet Benedict Joseph worked fearlessly and tirelessly by the side of his uncle to help those who were ill and to comfort those who had no hope of recovery. Eventually the boy's uncle, too, succumbed to the disease, and Benedict Joseph went to live with another uncle, who was also a priest. Here it was as if the future saint discovered a kindred soul. Abbé Vincent, his uncle, was absolutely selfless to the point where he has actually been compared to the Curé d'Ars. He lived in virtual and perpetual poverty, as all material goods that came his way were given in short order to the poor of his parish. Benedict Joseph and his uncle lived in a home that was little more than a hovel, and they often went without real food. Despite all this the boy was happy, and he felt close to Christ, whom he was sure was calling him constantly to the religious life, to a life of sacrifice, self-denial, and constant prayer.

As he entered his late teens Benedict Joseph was eager to do what he believed God wanted him to do. He wanted desperately to try his vocation, which he was sure was to the monastic life in one of its more severe forms. His first choice was the Trappists, and he yearned to go to their abbey and spend the rest of his life in prayer and work with them. His parents, however, were afraid for him to do so. They thought him too frail for the rigors of Trappist life. Apparently they hadn't been kept informed of the rigors their son had been enduring on a regular basis up to that point. Always unwilling to hurt or disappoint people in any way, Benedict Joseph did as they asked and applied instead for admission to the Carthusians, whose way of life, although very austere, was not as physically exacting as that of the Trappists.

After being referred by one charterhouse to another at Neuville, Benedict Joseph Labré arrived there eager to join. However, he soon learned, to his dismay, that his education was not sufficient to warrant entrance into the order. He was sent away to study logic and plainchant, something he tried mightily to do, although neither of the disciplines came easily to him. Eventually, however, he must have mastered these subjects well enough to satisfy the Carthusians because he finally was admitted as a postulant—for all of six weeks, at which point he was quickly and unambiguously sent away as unsuited to the religious life. Probably the boy was stung and disappointed. I imagine that he was very certain in his own mind of God's call to him, and it must have come as quite a blow that the Carthusians did not see that in him at all. He went home to Amettes but lost no time in applying to the Cistercians. He walked all the way to their abbey at La Trappe, and quickly discovered that he was more than four years too young to be considered for admittance.

Dejected, Benedict Joseph made his way on foot back to Amettes. He arrived several days later, dirty and physically exhausted, due not only to the ardors of the trip but the fact that he fasted during much of it. He stayed home for some time trying to decide the best course of action and then continued in his quest to enter the religious life. In total he attempted eleven times and was refused eleven times! Each time something went wrong. Sometimes his physical health seemed too weak; at others it is what we, today, would call his mental health that seemed a problem. In fact, it is very probable that it was the manifestation of certain psychological or even psychiatric symptoms that made him seem so unsuitable for the various religious communities to which he aspired. It must be remembered that the holiness of Benedict Joseph Labré was never in doubt. Indeed, many of the monks at the various monasteries to which he tried to gain entrance viewed him as saintly—but they also viewed him as definitely not monastic material.

It was at this point that Benedict Joseph Labré made the decision that would mark him as unique among the saints we are considering. He set out on foot to Rome, writing to his parents (in the one-and-only letter he was to send them) that he had decided to try his vocation in one of the monasteries of Italy. However, he never entered or even attempted to enter any of those mon-asteries, for somewhere along the way, as Benedict Joseph Labré walked the dusty roads from France to Rome, he came to the realization that he was different from other people and the destiny that God had set aside for him was different, as well. He came to realize that for him the comforts of the cloister were impossible and that he was called to an even more austere form of life than any enclosed monk. He believed he was called to wander, to have no home, no possessions, no security, to have no one but God on whom to rely. He believed that God was calling him to a life of penance, a life of total dependence on heaven.

If all of this reminds us of Saint Francis, Benedict Joseph Labré must have seen the similarity, as well, for he became a Franciscan tertiary and discarded the few possessions that he had, keeping only a couple of rosaries (one of which he wore around his neck), a crucifix, a breviary, a copy of *The Imitation of Christ,* and perhaps a few other religious books.

Maybe the idea of a wandering saint sounds somewhat roman-tic to you. If so, you should realize that this young man lived the same sort of life that homeless people in our large cities live today. He had no clothes other than whatever he was wearing at any given moment—usually a rough and not-very-clean robe. He had no food except that which he found. Benedict Joseph often begged just for a few morsels to keep himself alive. Yet, many times when he was given food or perhaps a few coins by some kind person, he would not use these things for himself; he would gave them to someone he thought needed them more than he did.

In truth he had nothing. Yet simultaneously he had a great deal, for this homeless, wandering saint who spent six years drift-ing from one great shrine to another and then the next six years on the streets of Rome had a closeness to God that few people can match and a compassion for others that is truly Christianity at its best. At times, exhausted and hungry, he yearned only to find a place to sleep; yet frequently he was told to move on, his dirty clothes and odd manner being disturbing to many. People such as Benedict Joseph Labré often make others uncomfortable; they show too clearly the fragility of life; they demonstrate how the lives we have built for ourselves can quickly crumble, leaving us with nothing to protect us.

In a way, however, Benedict Joseph Labré was living the life he had always envisioned for himself: he was living the life of a monk, but not a monk closed off from the world in a cloister. For Benedict Joseph Labré, the world was his cloister, and the holiness of his life was not hidden away behind thick walls but was on display for all who had eyes to see it. His holiness was apparent and inspiring. He became known as the "Saint of the Forty Hours" for his enormous devotion to the Blessed Sacrament and the long hours he spent in adoration before it. And the efforts of this man, who had nothing, to help others was a constant reminder that for the Christian, love of others must be a total giving of self.

Benedict Joseph Labré died at the age of thirty-five, probably from malnutrition. He collapsed on the streets of Rome, as many homeless, poverty-stricken people have done over many centuries. Yet his death was a wrenching experience for those who knew him, for his very odd life had affected many people deeply and shown them what true love of God looks like. In the first chapter of this little book we called Saint Ignatius of Antioch an "athlete of God." Here I am tempted to call Saint Benedict Joseph Labré a "clown of God." The life he lived was strange and should have been deeply sad. Yet ultimately it was not sad but joyous; this wandering monk shows us that the values of the world count for nothing, and that real happiness comes only from love of God and others.

Wonderings and Wanderings with Saint Benedict Joseph Labré

Meals in a novitiate—at least when I was in one—were rather different from meals in other places. Someone was always appointed to read edifying works to us as we ate, for it was considered important that we not waste time, that we use all the hours of the day to draw closer to God. When I was seventeen and a novice with the Capuchins, the book that was read evening after evening was *Saints for Sinners,* by Archbishop Alban Goodier, S.J. It was interesting and I was very attentive to the reading. I liked hearing about the various saints, but something special seemed to happen to me when the section on Saint Benedict Joseph Labré was being read. I was startled and deeply moved by this saint, perhaps because I had always been told by my parents and the sisters who were my teachers in school that it was important to be available to those in need. I had even met some hobos (for that is what we called them years ago) in my hometown, and had been able to give them some food or perhaps a little money. I was amazed to find that a man who was like these hobos had actually become a saint. I think that during the reading of this section of Archbishop Goodier's book my understanding of sainthood changed and broadened somewhat, and I eventually started thinking an odd thought. I began to think that this hobo saint would somehow be very important to me and that perhaps I would even take his name, for we were soon to choose our names in religious life. And so I did, and so he has been.

After I made my vows and was known as Brother Benedict Joseph, one of my first tasks made me think of the hobo saint again. I was assigned to take care of the homeless men who came to the Capuchin monastery in Garrison, New York. We didn't house such men, but the Franciscan Friars of the Atonement at Graymoor, who were very close by, were famous for giving hobos and the like a place to stay for several weeks. We turned out to be the last meal on the way to Graymoor for many of these men. In this way I began to take care of homeless men, who turned out to be a fascinating and colorful group. Among them were people with doctorates and people who could speak rare and unusual languages, people who seemed to have fallen from a world of privilege to one of destitution. As a young man I wondered how such a thing could happen, and I found myself praying to Saint Benedict Joseph Labré for these men. I remember one man saying to me: "There's something wrong with every one of us if we can't take care of ourselves." It hurt to hear those words, but I knew they were true. I wondered about the patron I had chosen. Had he been unable to take care of himself? Had there been any place like Graymoor to help him?

I thought long and hard about the life of Saint Benedict Joseph Labré. What had made him so different from others? There is no sign that he chose the life of a wanderer. But it was clear that he simply couldn't fit in at the various monasteries he tried to join. Something buried deep within him, something that we can only speculate about, prevented him from living the kind of life most people lead. It kept him from fulfilling his dream of becoming a monk. So he kept walking, wandering alone from shrine to shrine, making himself a monk of the roads. He went every summer to the great shrine of Saint James at Compostela, actually crossing the Pyrenees Mountains on foot. Along the way until fairly recent times there were little inns named after Saint Benedict Joseph Labré along the routes he had traveled. This little man who fit in nowhere managed to leave his name in places of considerable importance, which shows that despite whatever emotional or psychological problems he may have had, he affected people deeply. Statues of him can be found in Loretto and in Compostela. Incidentally, a statue of him is in our own National Shrine of the Immaculate Conception in Washington, DC. He stands with a number of other saints who were dedicated to the Blessed Sacrament.

What does such a life teach us today? I believe Saint Benedict Joseph Labré offers us much to ponder, and I believe that he challenges us, perhaps in ways we do not like to be challenged. Our world likes perfection—or what it imagines to be perfection. We do not like those with disabilities or psychiatric problems. They show too clearly the frailty of human life, the many things that can go wrong with our bodies and our minds. They remind us of our own imperfections, the ones we work so hard to conceal even from those closest to us. We want to marginalize such people, to get them out of sight. The life of Saint Benedict Joseph Labré teaches us that God does not agree with us in this. Despite his serious psychological shortcomings Saint Benedict Joseph Labré was loved by God just as we all are. And Benedict Joseph loved God in return even though his life hadn't turned out the way he had planned it. He also loved others, and he did the best he could. Whatever there was of this poor man, he offered it completely to God, and this is the definition of holiness. Can any of us say we do the same?

Our world, while congratulating itself endlessly on its tolerance, rejects difference. I wonder sometimes what we would make of Saint Francis today. I think we would probably shun him as we would shun Saint Benedict Joseph Labré. Yet only about one hundred twenty years ago a very sophisticated man, Pope Leo XIII, canonized Benedict Joseph. Pope Leo could see the holiness that the grime and dirt of Benedict Joseph's many wanderings would have concealed from us. He could see that sainthood does not have to be paired with perfection. The Pope said about him at this time *"admirablis sed non usus,"* which means admirable but not imitable. This is true in one sense: we certainly should not want to live our lives as vagabonds like Saint Benedict Joseph Labré. I don't know that it is true in all senses, however, for there is much to imitate in this little hobo: his love and his acceptance of the will of God in his life are two good examples. The Pope was certainly right that we should admire this saint. In fact, our admiration of him should be great, as should our admiration of all who struggle against handicaps, whether psychological or physical.

Saint Benedict Joseph Labré reminds me of the saints of the ancient Egyptian desert. Like them he was different. Like them his difference from others did not mean that he was incapable of achieving extraordinary holiness, the holiness of a real saint. As someone who has carried this gentle and wonderful saint's name for sixty years, I can't help but feel that somehow he got dropped off in the wrong century and would have done very well in the third or fourth century (sometimes I feel that way about myself, as well). But he lived at a time when his life was a struggle and this is the same struggle we see on our city streets nearly every day.

I chose the name of this saint when I was seventeen years old and have tried to be worthy of it. There is not one moment since that time that I have regretted my decision.

━━━

It is hardly surprising that a saint like Benedict Joseph Labré did not leave behind a great many writings. He did, however, leave us a beautiful blessing which I would like to share with you. He used to say this to all those who helped him:

Jesus Christ, the King of glory, came in peace
God was made man.
The Word was made flesh
Christ was born of the Virgin Mary.
Christ passed through the midst of them in peace
Christ was crucified.
Christ died.
Christ was buried.
Christ is risen.
Christ ascended into heaven.
Christ conquers, Christ reigns, Christ commands.
From every lightning bolt may Christ defend us.
Jesus is with us.[1]

I can't help including two sayings of Saint Benedict Joseph Labré that I've always loved. They just seem to cut to the heart of things:

Those only are to be called poor and unhappy who are in hell, who have lost God for eternity, not those who are poor on earth.

And:

A little suffices to support the body; what is superfluous will only serve to furnish the worms a greater feast.

14.

SAINT CATHERINE LABOURÉ

IT IS A LITTLE DIFFICULT to imagine a Catholic who has never heard of the Miraculous Medal. Many of us have worn these medals around our necks since childhood. In fact, we've worn them so long that we may have forgotten the first time we put one on. The Miraculous Medal is not just another religious article; it is special to us in ways we cannot always easily articulate, and it gives us a real feeling of closeness to our Blessed Mother. The image of her on this medal is probably the way most of us think of her. Here she stands on top of the world. A serpent coils beneath her feet—a serpent she effortlessly pins down and renders harmless and helpless. Rays of light stream from her hands, reminding us, perhaps, of the rays that stream from the heart of Jesus in the image of the Divine Mercy. In this image of Mary she is certainly "full of grace." She is indeed miraculous. She is unquestionably the Queen of Heaven and Earth.

The Miraculous Medal has been a great gift to Catholics, but it is so much a part of our lives that we often don't think of its origins, of how we came to have this remarkable medal through the visions of a young French religious sister nearly two centuries ago. So I thought it was about time to examine the life of Saint Catherine Labouré, a Daughter of Charity, a visionary, the saint through whom we received this treasure we call the Miraculous Medal.

The Secret Saint of the Miraculous Medal

The first thing we should know about Catherine Labouré is that she was not baptized Catherine, nor was she ever called that until she entered religious life. Her name was Zoé, which is a Greek word that means "life." She was born in 1806 in a town called Fain-le-Moutiers in the burgundy region of France. Her family was even larger than was typical at the time, and Zoé Labouré was the ninth of seventeen children, of whom eleven survived to adulthood. Like so many people who develop vibrant and devout inner lives, Zoé encountered tragedy and sorrow at an early age. Her mother died when the girl was only nine years old. Such a loss has an incalculable effect on one so young, and children who lose a parent often try to find a substitute. In Zoé Labouré's case, the choice of substitute was prophetic. It is said that after her mother's funeral, the little girl picked up a statue of the Blessed Mother, and as she kissed it said: "Now you will be my mother."[1]

Relatively little is known about the rest of Saint Catherine Labouré's childhood. We do know that a loving aunt took the little girl and her younger sister to live with her in a town not far away and that little Zoé was well cared for there. We also know that when she was old enough she returned to her father's house and there took over managing the household. Now it was her turn to care for others as her aunt had cared for her, and this she did well. From all we can tell this future saint seemed a responsible and gentle young woman, very concerned with the needs of others.

A deep prayerfulness developed in Zoé Labouré, as well as an ever-increasing attachment to our Lady. Clearly these had to find some mode of expression as the girl grew up. One of her older sisters had become a Daughter of Charity of Saint Vincent de Paul, and as Zoé entered her teens she began to contemplate doing the same. One night she had a dream of an elderly priest who was tending to the sick. He told her: "God has designs on you—do not forget it." Sometime later she visited a hospital operated by the Daughters of Charity. On the wall was a portrait, and when Zoé looked at it closely, she was certain that it was the priest she had seen in her dream. The portrait was of Saint Vincent de Paul, founder of the Daughters of Charity. Zoé took this to be a sign and began to make plans to enter the order.

Her father was brokenhearted. Zoé was his favorite child, and the thought of losing her to the religious life was something he simply was not ready to accept. So, putting her father's needs before her own, Zoé stayed at home until she was twenty-four years old. When at last she entered the Daughters of Charity, she began to see possibilities of happiness that had been unknown to her since her mother's death. At the time of her first vows, she took the name Catherine, the name by which everyone knows her today.

God works differently in the lives of different saints. He offers radically different paths to different people. Visionaries, while not rare, are certainly not among the majority of saints. Yet this is the special grace that was granted to Sister Catherine Labouré. She was not long in the convent before she is said to have experienced things that were far from the ordinary. At one point for three consecutive days she "saw" the heart of Saint Vincent de Paul above the reliquary in which his relics were kept. These are her words on the matter:

> The first day the heart was white symbolizing peace, calm innocence and union. On the second day it appeared to be red like the charity, which must enflame our hearts. I sensed that the Community would undergo renewal and would spread throughout the world. Finally on the last day it was black. This distressed me greatly. I do not know why, nor do I know if this sadness was related to the revolution that

would soon take place. I spoke to my confessor who tried to calm me as much as possible, and distract me from all these thoughts.[2]

Not long after this she wrote again about another vision, this one of Christ in the Eucharist. Again we turn to her own words:

> I was also favored with another great grace, that of seeing Our Lord in the Blessed Sacrament. This happened throughout my time in the novitiate until I allowed myself to doubt. After this I saw nothing because I had doubted this profound mystery, and I believed that I may have been mistaken in what I had seen.[3]

While it is tempting to take these words at face value we ought never to jump to conclusions, for it is not always possible to distinguish between pious legend and supernatural experience. We ought also to remember that in the case of a young and very devout person like Sister Catherine Labouré, whose personality tended to be that of a romantic and a dreamer, the role of imagination may play a part in such experiences. This is not to say there was nothing supernatural going on; it is only to say that private revelations always come to us through the filter, the prism, of a specific personality and a specific personal history.

No matter what we conclude regarding these early "mystical experiences," the fact is that Sister Catherine Labouré was not long in the religious life before the apparitions that would make her known throughout the world began. These visions are detailed and elaborate, very different from those of that other famous French visionary, Bernadette Soubirous, at whom we shall look soon. The first of Catherine Labouré's visions occurred on July 18, 1830. The other sisters were asleep when Catherine was awakened by the voice of a child calling her. She dressed and followed the child, who led her to the sisters' chapel. There she experienced a vision of our Lady that went on for over two hours. This was not, however, an experience simply of the presence of our Lady. There was a type of communication that Saint Catherine later spoke and wrote of as if it were simple speech. In fact, she seems to have talked with our Lady for most of the two hours as the Blessed Mother sat in a chair in the chapel. Catherine heard the Virgin Mary say to her, "God wishes to charge you with a mission. You will be contradicted, but do not fear; you will have the grace to do what is necessary. Tell your spiritual director all that passes within you. Times are evil in France and in the world."[4]

Four months later, on the evening of November 27, 1830, Catherine was again in the chapel, deep in prayer, when without any warning she discovered herself once again in the presence of the Blessed Mother. Catherine's first vision seemed to center on words—the auditory; this vision—intensely dramatic—was far more visual. And it is from this vision that we find the image which became known as the Miraculous Medal. This time our Lady was revealed to Catherine as standing inside an oval frame-like structure, with her feet on a globe. Her fingers were adorned with many rings of different colors and from these rings streamed rays of intense light. Around the oval appeared the words that have become known to Catholics throughout the world: "O Mary, conceived without sin, pray for us who have recourse to thee."[5] Transfixed, Catherine watched, and the frame within which Mary stood seemed to rotate, revealing a circle of twelve stars, the letter M, and a cross. Beneath these were the Sacred Heart of Jesus and the Immaculate Heart of Mary. And thus, on that night, the miraculous medal was first envisioned. Catherine then heard Mary instruct her to tell her confessor about the images she had just seen and to have them engraved on medals. Our Lady also said that those who wore these medals would receive great graces. This vision, or at least visions very similar to it, came to Catherine over and over again during the next few months.

The extravagance of Catherine's visions makes them somewhat difficult for modern readers, who chafe at their specificity.

We want and expect such mystical experiences to exceed the bounds of language. In other words, we want something that cannot easily be translated into words or images. We are not necessarily wrong in this, and these same problems occurred to Father Aladel, the priest to whom Catherine confided her experiences. Yet after careful investigation he could find nothing improper about them, and Catherine's sincerity was without the smallest doubt. Therefore he allowed the first miraculous medals, faithful copies of what she had seen, to be made.

The medals quickly became popular, and their presence around the necks of more and more people in France drew the attention of many. One man who developed a keen interest in them was the Archbishop of Paris, who in 1836 began a canonical inquiry into the visions that had produced the medals. He had one big problem in doing this, however, and that was that he had no idea who the visionary was. Catherine Labouré had taken great pains to exact a promise from her confessor that he would not reveal who had seen the vision of the medal, and the priest had complied faithfully. Despite all this, the inquiry was decided in favor of the mysterious visionary—even without Saint Catherine ever entering into it. The medals themselves were approved by the highest French ecclesiastical authority.

If the Miraculous Medal needed any more publicity, it surely got it in 1842, when Aphonse Ratisbonne, a Jewish man from Alsace, was somehow persuaded to wear one. While wearing the medal he had his own vision of our Lady, which transformed his life, brought him to the baptismal font, then the priesthood, and eventually to founding a religious order, the Fathers and Sisters of Sion. All of France seemed in the grip of the visions of Sister Catherine Labouré. Yet, still, no one knew who she was.

Saint Catherine Labouré lived until the very last day of 1876. She spent those years as she wanted to spend them: in absolute obscurity. Until only a few months before her death no one but the faithful Father Aladel knew of her visions or that she was the source of the Miraculous Medal. She lived the life of an unassuming member of her religious congregation, caring for the elderly, being portress at her convent, and even for a time taking care of the chickens and ducks at her convent. She had encountered the Mother of God, yet lived as if nothing special had ever happened to her. Her death, however, brought her the fame that she avoided during her life, and there was a great outpouring of love and countless people offered Sister Catherine Labouré the veneration one usually reserves for a canonized saint.

In Saint Catherine Labouré we have a saint somewhat different from those we have examined so far. We have a romantic young woman of unusual and precise visions. Perhaps we even have a woman who would have been considered delusional in our own time. Yet we also have a hidden saint who shunned the fame her visions would easily have given her. We have a peasant girl who was given by God the gift of heralding to the world a Marian doctrine which the Church had not yet even finished defining. Through Saint Catherine Labouré we have been given the Miraculous Medal, a source of many miracles, a comfort to countless Catholics, and a great aid to the faith of many. Without this hidden Daughter of Charity, the Church in the last two centuries would have been very different.

FROM NOVENAS IN NEW JERSEY TO PRAYING IN THE RUE DU BAC

Starting in about the seventh grade I went to the Miraculous Medal Novena in my family's parish in New Jersey. I remember it as being a very well attended service. A good percentage of the parish could be counted on to be there, and there were people of all ages and backgrounds. It was part of parish life, and I attended almost every week right up until the week before I left to begin my novitiate. This novena was beautiful. I can still remember the lovely hymns that were sung to our Lady. Thinking about it gives me a real feeling of nostalgia. To show you how long ago this was, in the novena prayers we always called Catherine Labouré "Blessed." She had not yet been canonized. Of course we all wore Miraculous Medals. Back then it seemed there was hardly a Catholic in the country who didn't wear one.

I never stopped wearing my Miraculous Medal, and many years later I had the opportunity to go to Paris. While most people on their first trip to that lovely city head to the Louvre or the Eiffel Tower, I had a different destination in mind and—map in hand—found my way to the rue du Bac. I wanted to be in the place that our Lady appeared to Saint Catherine Labouré, where she gave this retiring saint the design for the medal that was so important to us. I found myself in a decent-size chapel, and I was glad that it was fairly large, as it was rather crowded. There were a good number of Asians, whom I assumed to be mostly Filipinos. I was pleased that I wasn't the only one in Paris who was interested in the Miraculous Medal, but I must admit I would have liked a little more privacy as I tried to pray. Eventually I worked my way to the front of the chapel, and there it was: the chair in which Saint Catherine Labouré said our Lady sat. It was slightly strange to look at this chair, an ordinary piece of furniture that was used by such an extraordinary guest. It was cordoned off so no one could touch it, let alone sit on it. Not far away, right at the edge of the altar, was Saint Catherine's body, which is incorrupt. As I stood there I felt the presence of our Lady, and I found myself in unexpectedly deep prayer to her. This is a trip I have never forgotten.

The sophistication of our time ignores or scoffs at mystical events. I never have. In fact, I am inclined to be very cynical when it comes to cynics, and I was deeply moved by visiting this chapel. Right nearby, one could visit the mother house of the Vincentians, which contains the tomb of Saint Vincent de Paul. The holiness of the lives associated with these places was almost palpable.

I have always been attracted to those few people in the history of the Church who have been privileged to experience a vision of our Lady. I am fascinated by the fact that they are always so unassuming, so young and innocent. Although a little older than Bernadette and the children at Fatima, Saint Catherine Labouré, nonetheless, has a similar quality. She is as artless as a child, and I believe it is this that makes her open to experiencing the holy; she is a child experiencing the presence of a mother. In her case, however, it is no ordinary mother; it is the Mother of God. In Saint Catherine's descriptions of her visions there are times when she believed she placed her hands in our Lady's lap or was embraced by our Lady. In our day we wonder if such a thing is possible. Saint Catherine Labouré didn't wonder; she simply accepted the presence of our Lady, and so was able to bring the Miraculous Medal to the world.

Saint Catherine Labouré has been part of my life since the first day I went to those old-style novenas back in New Jersey. And, by the way, those novena prayers are still part of my life. Her visions have become my own, just as they have become the property of many, for when I picture the Mother of God, I picture her in the way that Saint Catherine Labouré saw her. Saint Catherine Labouré was the gateway through which a great gift came into the world; the medal that we call miraculous is well named. It has strengthened the faith of countless people, and brought innumerable people to Jesus through His Blessed Mother.

I urge you if at all possible to go to Paris. It's all right if you go to the Louvre and even the Eiffel Tower, as long as you don't forget to go to Notre Dame and to Sacré Coeur. Then take the Metro to the station called Babylon. It has this unusual name because the early Vincentians had gone to Babylon as missionaries. Walk to the chapel in the rue du Bac, and when you're there gaze upon a chair used by the Mother of God, and pray in a place where our Lady appeared to a young Daughter of Charity. While you're doing this you might want to hold your Miraculous Medal and thank our Lady and Saint Catherine Labouré for the great treasure you have in your hand.

═════

As you may suspect, the retiring visionary of the rue du Bac did not leave many writings for us to contemplate. So instead of looking at anything Saint Catherine Labouré wrote, we will look at something written about her. Following are the words of Pope Pius XII, which he spoke at her canonization. We see in them the simplicity that is so often found in the truly holy.

Favored though she was with visions and celestial delights, she did not advertise herself to seek worldly fame, but took herself merely for the handmaid of God and preferred to remain unknown and to be reported as nothing. And thus desiring only the glory of God and of His Mother, she went meekly about the ordinary and even unpleasant tasks that were assigned to her in the bosom of her religious family.

She was always willing and ready to give diligent attentions to the sick, ministering to their bodies and their souls; to wait upon the old and the infirm without sparing herself; to act as portress, receiving all with a serene and modest countenance; to cook; to mend torn and tattered clothing; to carry out, in a word, all the duties laid upon her, even the unattractive and onerous ones. And while she worked away, never idle but always busy and cheerful, her heart never lost sight of heavenly things: indeed she saw God uninterruptedly in all things and all things in God.

Impelled by the urging of love, she hurried eagerly before the tabernacle as often as she could, or before the sacred image of her holy Mother, to pour out the desires of her heart and to make an offering of the fragrance of her prayers. Accordingly, it was evident that while she dwelt in earthly exile, in mind and heart she lived in Heaven and sought, before everything else, to mount with rapid steps to the highest perfection, and to spend all her powers in reaching it. She loved the Sacred Heart of Jesus and the Immaculate Heart of Mary with a special warmth of piety; and she was ever on the watch to influence, by word and example, as many other persons as she could to love Them.

And thus when she came to the end of her mortal life, she did not face death with fear but with gladness. Confident in God and the most Holy Virgin, she took time to distribute, with a weak and tremulous hand, the last of her Miraculous Medals to those standing by, and then, content and smiling, she hastened away to heaven.[6]

15.

SAINT BERNADETTE SOUBIROUS

MANY YEARS AGO, AT A moment when I was feeling very discouraged, Blessed Mother Teresa of Calcutta asked me a question I could not answer. She asked why I thought God had chosen me to be a priest. It seems a simple question, but I was caught off guard, and to be honest, I was stumped. I mumbled something rather foolish in response, something she wisely ignored. She then said some words I will never forget: "You are chosen because of the humility of God. God chooses the weakest and the poorest, the most inappropriate persons to use." Mother Teresa was absolutely right. We can see the truth of her words wherever we look, among clergy, religious—even saints. I believe we see this truth in a special way in the case of the saint we will now consider.

Bernadette Soubirous was a humble, barely literate peasant girl. The town in which she lived was such a backwater in France that the population didn't even speak the French language, using instead a dialect called Gascon that was more similar to Spanish. She seemed neither very intelligent nor destined for anything special. Bernadette Soubirous was exactly the sort of person the world looks down on or simply ignores. Yet she was chosen by God for a deep mystical encounter with His Blessed Mother, and she was chosen to bring a miracle of hope and healing into the world.

The Peasant Saint Who Met Our Lady

The girl we call Saint Bernadette of Lourdes was born on January 7, 1844. She was given the name Marie-Bernarde but apparently was almost never called by this name, preferring the diminutive form, Bernadette, instead. Her father, François, a miller, was not only a poor businessman but an unlucky one. He lost his mill and his livelihood when Bernadette was only a child. Thus began a long, steady spiral into poverty for the Soubirous family, forcing Louise, Bernadette's mother, to support the family as a laundress. A weak child, Bernadette was plagued by illness for most of her life; as a toddler she survived cholera, but this early ailment left her afflicted with respiratory problems for the rest of her life. Even though she was not strong, Bernadette cared very lovingly for her four younger siblings[1] while her mother was out of the home working.

Primarily because of ill health, Bernadette began her education late, and at the age of fourteen she was still doing very elementary work in a class surrounded by seven-year-olds. The sisters who taught her were of the opinion that Bernadette had little aptitude for studies. She was actually lucky to be able to go to school at all because by that time her family's financial situation had worsened to the point where they had all moved to one room in the cellar of a local building. This room actually had once been a prison cell and was still called *le cachot*, which means the dungeon—hardly an appealing place for a family of seven to live.

Like most children of the time, Bernadette had certain tasks to perform to help the family. One of these was the collection of firewood. On February 11, 1858, when she was still only fourteen, Bernadette was on one of her expeditions into the countryside to find wood. With her were her younger sister Toinette and a friend named Marie Abadie. Nothing seemed to distinguish this day from any other. When the girls arrived at a grotto with an icy stream, the two other girls took off their shoes and socks to wade through the water, but Bernadette lagged behind, worried that the cold might aggravate her health problems. Finally she began to remove her shoes, but before she had done so, her life changed forever. This is the way she described what happened:

> Scarcely had I removed my first stocking when I heard a noise like a gust of wind. When I turned my head towards the prairie, I saw the trees quiet, not swaying at all, so I began removing my stockings again. I heard the same noise again. When I raised my head and looked at the grotto, I saw a Lady in white. She was wearing a white gown with a blue sash, a white veil and a golden rose on each foot, the same color as the chain of her Rosary, which had white beads.[2]

And in this simple way, the little peasant girl experienced what, since the Assumption, no pope or bishop ever had—the presence of our Lady.

What must Bernadette have thought? What must she have felt? Her experience in life was so limited, it is hard to imagine that she could have had any inkling of what was really happening. Her response, again in her own words, is both charmingly innocent and absolutely right. She removed her rosary beads from her pocket and sank to her knees: "The Lady let me pray alone; she passed the beads of the rosary between her fingers, but said nothing; only at the end of each decade did she say the Gloria with me."[3]

It is unclear how long her prayer in the presence of our Lady went on, but after it was done the mysterious woman in white disappeared into the grotto and Bernadette was soon found by the other girls. On their way home she told them of her vision, swearing them to secrecy—a promise they made and then promptly broke, as most children would.

Only three days later Bernadette was back at the grotto with several of her friends. Again she experienced the presence of the beautiful woman in white. Although her friends saw nothing except Bernadette in deep and serene prayer, when they returned to Lourdes they told of Bernadette's strange visions, and soon the village was speaking of nothing else.

Four days later Bernadette returned to the grotto. At this point the woman in white asked her to come every day for two weeks, which she did, and each time she was met by the mysterious woman. Soon crowds of people were accompanying her, hoping to encounter something miraculous. But it was only Bernadette who perceived the woman. Despite the interest of so many people, Bernadette's parents were embarrassed by their daughter, ashamed that she seemed to be seeing things that were not there. Perhaps she had lost her mind. Perhaps her visions came from the devil. The local police, suspecting a hoax, questioned Bernadette, but she stood firm, stubbornly asserting the reality of her visions and the goodness of the woman.

During one of her visits, the vision told her, "You will pray for sinners." During another, the mysterious lady asked her to dig in a certain place with her hands. When Bernadette did so, she unearthed a tiny spring, which grew into a steady stream. This is the water that even today people journey from all over the world to bathe in, for this is the water that has produced inexplicable cures and strengthened the faith of many.

The visions at the grotto continued. On one occasion the lady told Bernadette that a chapel should be built and a procession begun. When Bernadette relayed this information to the local priest and others, she was met with hostility and a demand that the lady of her vision identify herself. Disbelief was everywhere. Most people were divided as to whether Bernadette was delusional or a liar. At the same time susceptible people in the area were beginning to believe they, too, were seeing visions. It seemed as if this one young girl were throwing the whole town into chaos.

On March 25, the Feast of the Annunciation, Bernadette had her most famous encounter with our Lady, for that was the day she asked the mysterious woman her name. The answer mystified the young peasant girl. What was she to make of the woman's response? What sense could she derive from the statement "I am the Immaculate Conception"?[4] Yet when she reported the woman's words to the priests and townspeople, she was met with awe and excitement. What some people had believed to be true now seemed incontrovertible: The woman whom Bernadette had seen was Mary, the Mother of God.

Bernadette had only two more visions at the grotto, one on April 7 and the other on July 16. By this time swarms of people had been caught up in the idea of Bernadette's visions and the authorities barricaded the grotto to prevent crowds from gathering there. Even this did not stop word of Bernadette's miraculous visions from spreading throughout France, and the demand became great that the grotto be opened to the public. Finally it was; and, one by one, cures began to be reported, attributed to the water of the spring that Bernadette had unearthed at our Lady's command.

The cures came and continue to come—a sign of the truth of Bernadette's visions and the infinite power of God—but Bernadette never again experienced the presence of our Lady in this life. Yet the memory of those encounters was with her at every second. It seems that she was drawn from that point onward to a life of prayer and contemplation, but she had become famous—a celebrity. Peace and privacy became difficult for her and her family, as people from all over Europe came to see the visionary. Finally, at the age of twenty-two she joined the Sisters of Charity and Christian Instruction, who had been her childhood teachers.

Bernadette's time in the convent was not easy. Fearing that the famous young girl from Lourdes would expect special treatment, the novice mistress and other sisters went out of their way to give her just the opposite. Perhaps at times they were even cruel to her. By the time she made her final vows at the age of twenty-four, Bernadette was ill. Still, people came to her, hoping to hear her stories of the Blessed Mother. Each one of these interviews was very taxing for her. Yet she put up with them as she put up with every other cross she was offered. Our Lady had told her she would not attain happiness in this life, and this was something she accepted with unwavering trust. Bernadette's illnesses worsened; she developed a malignant tumor on her leg and a series of other ailments. Sickness seemed to follow her so much that she once said that she had no other purpose but to "suffer." Finally on April 16, 1879, at the age of thirty-five she was released from the pain of earthly life and entered the joy of heaven. Her last words were: "Blessed Mary, Mother of God, pray for me! A poor sinner . . ."

In Bernadette of Lourdes we have a great reminder that we do not see as God sees, that earthly greatness and spiritual greatness are very different from each other. In choosing this pious little peasant girl for so intimate an encounter with His Blessed Mother, God reveals to us His love for the littlest among us, the importance of every human life. He reveals, as well, His mysterious humility. In Bernadette of Lourdes we have a wonderful example of what Mother Teresa called "the weakest and the poorest, the most inappropriate persons to use." Yet we also have an example of a saint who has inspired countless people and will continue to do so for centuries to come.

THE GRACE OF COURAGE

Many years ago, when I was about ten years old, a movie premiered. Called *The Song of Bernadette,* it told the story of the little visionary of Lourdes, Bernadette Soubirous. This was during those last days before television took over, before moving images had invaded our homes, and movies still had a great impact. Going to them was a significant event. This movie, however, was of special importance because it not only had a Catholic theme; it dealt with a miracle that fascinated just about everyone: the apparition of the Blessed Mother to a young French girl and the sign left by our Lady; the miraculous spring at Lourdes, which has been the source of countless miracles of healing. Both Catholics and non-Catholics flocked to the theaters to see *The Song of Bernadette*, and—my ten-year-old self in tow—my family was among them. This film made a deep impression on me, as it did on many Catholic children of the time. It formed my ideas concerning Bernadette Soubirous and her mystical experiences with the Mother of God. It also had an effect on my idea of what a saint should be.

In that movie the part of Bernadette was played by a young actress named Jennifer Jones, who was twenty-four, ten years older than Bernadette was at the time of her visions. Jennifer Jones was beautiful and even ethereal. For years this was my impression of Bernadette, but as I began reading more about her and praying to her I realized that the little French peasant girl who saw our Lady was very different from the actress who portrayed her. Bernadette was certainly a saint, but she was not ethereal. She was very much flesh and blood and very much down-to-earth.

Bernadette, who experienced several celestial visions of our Lady, came from a life of extreme poverty, a life that offered little future. We would like to imagine that these visions would have changed her life for the better. In fact, they did not make her life easier. If anything, they made things more difficult. Saint Catherine Labouré was able to keep her identity as a visionary hidden from the world and to live in peaceful seclusion. But from the very beginning Bernadette was forced to confront the world without any protection. And she faced it far better than most of us could have done. Think of it for a moment: a young peasant girl, who was barely in her teens and had almost no education, was dealing with many people who thought she was a liar. Others were convinced that she was mad. Still others imagined that she was only trying to attract attention to herself. We think of skepticism as something indigenous to our own time. It is not. There were plenty of skeptics in Bernadette's time who scoffed at the very idea of her visions. Bernadette was actually interrogated by the police and none too politely. They were determined to make her say that she had made up stories about visions.

But she did not say anything of the kind. She stood her ground. She did not doubt her own experience. She did not change one detail of her accounts regarding her miraculous visions. She did not doubt what God, through His Blessed Mother, was telling her.

We are all heavily influenced by the thoughts and expectations of others. Our idea of the possible and the impossible is largely formed by the culture in which we live, by the countless voices that constantly tell us what is real and what is not, what to think and what not to think. As a psychologist I would say that it should have been very easy to convince an unlettered girl like Bernadette that she did not see what she thought she had seen, that such things are impossible. Many tried but no one was able to convince Bernadette of this. She remained serenely secure—not in herself (which would have been mere pride) but in God and His Blessed Mother. She was anchored by this in a way that few of us would be, protected from doubting the overwhelming events that she had experienced.

How rare that is in our world. How rare it is to find someone for whom the reality of God is more powerful than the reality of the world that rejects God. I am in awe of the strength of this young girl who endured so much ridicule and rejection and yet stood firm. Even after she had entered a convent, she was often treated with less than kindness. At times she must have felt abandoned; yet she never lost faith in her visions; she never despaired. Bernadette possessed a serenity amid turmoil, a granite-like conviction in the reality of her visions that enabled her to withstand the constant chipping away at faith, in which the world is always engaged. How often I pray to her for the grace to disregard the ideas that the world perpetually bombards us with and to listen instead to the "still small voice" of God.

The strength and faith of a Saint Bernadette should not astound us; it should embarrass us, because our own faith is so tepid by comparison. When it comes to our own willingness to stand up for God and the Church without changing one iota of the truth, we are weak compared with her. When we are tempted to give in, to modify our beliefs to make them palatable to the world, we should remember this little peasant girl who stood firm against everyone and stood alone.

In the *The Song of Bernadette* I saw an ethereal saint enraptured by her visions of the Mother of God. In Bernadette Soubirous I met a flesh-and-blood young girl who was a great saint, who held on to her faith—her visions—no matter what the world said or did.

━━━

What more important writing can there be from the pen of Bernadette Soubirous than a description of her visions? Following is a brief description she wrote of her first encounter with the Blessed Mother.

When I first saw her, I was a little bit afraid. Thinking that what I was seeing was an illusion, I rubbed my eyes, but it made no difference: I still saw the same Lady. So I put my hand in my pocket and took out my Rosary. I tried in vain to make the sign of the cross; I was not able to raise my hand to my forehead. When I realized this, I froze completely in fear. The Lady took the Rosary she was holding between her hands and she made the sign of the cross. Then I tried a second time and this time I was able to do it. Immediately after I had made the sign of the cross, the great fear that had seized me disappeared. I knelt and prayed the Rosary, in the presence of this beautiful Lady. She passed the beads of her Rosary between her fingers, but she did not move her lips. When I finished praying the Rosary, she made a sign to me to draw near to her, but I did not dare. Then she suddenly disappeared.[5]

16.

Saint Thérèse of Lisieux

CAN YOU THINK OF a more recognizable or beloved saint than the Little Flower? This quiet nun, who died at the age of twenty-four, exerts a tremendous attraction on us, and she's done so for at least a century. Many throughout the world are devoted to her, but how many of us really understand her? Pope Benedict XVI (as Cardinal Ratzinger) once called her "[t]hat lovable saint . . . who looks so naive and unproblematical."[1] The pope's point is that Thérèse only appears "naive," and he goes on to show that there is far more depth in the Little Flower than many people realize.

I agree with the pope that we often perceive Thérèse superficially. That's not surprising, because it's the way her statues and holy cards portray her: as a lovely, smiling, serene young woman in the brown habit and flowing white mantle of the Carmelites. We are all familiar with the multitude of roses that seem to tumble from her hands like gifts for us. But do we sometimes overlook the fact that she carries not just flowers but the Cross of Christ? Do we forget sometimes that the many blessings in this wonderful saint's life were counterbalanced by trials and difficulties, some of them beginning when she was a small child? Would we rather not know that at the end of her earthly life she endured not only great pain but a strong temptation to despair, a temptation to imagine that beyond death lies only nothingness?

I fear that we want to make Thérèse a plaster saint, one who lived a life of tranquility and untroubled intimacy with God. She is not. The short life of this great saint, most of which was lived either surrounded by a loving, devout family or in the cloister, was the life of a valiant woman in love with God. She experienced not only the blessedness of intense devotion but the agonizing sense of estrangement and uncertainty that marks our own era. Saint Thérèse of Lisieux died when she was little more than a girl, yet she became a Doctor of the Church, and I believe she has much to say to us if we would only listen.

The Saint Who Is Loved by the Whole World

One might be tempted to think that Thérèse was born for saintliness or even that her sanctity was somehow genetic. Her parents, Louis Martin and Zélie Guérin Martin, were a devout and loving couple who were absolutely devoted to God, the Church, and their family. Their holiness was so unmistakable that in 2008 Pope Benedict XVI beatified them both, making it possible that there will one day be three canonized saints from the same family. Perhaps we find so much devotion to God concentrated in such a small group of people impossible to understand, but if that is so, it is a sad commentary on us and our disbelieving age.

Thérèse's father came from a military family but felt drawn to the religious life. An attempt to join the Canons of Saint Augustine in the French Alps (famous, among other things, for their Saint Bernard dogs), however, ended in failure and Louis Martin moved to Alençon, about one hundred miles west of Paris, to become a watchmaker, a trade at which he had much success. There he met Zélie Guérin. She also came from a military family background, one that was almost devoid of love and affection, and perhaps it was this lack in her early life that helped Zélie become so loving and compassionate toward her own family. Like her husband-to-be, she had tried religious life and failed. It is almost as if God had other plans for them. Coming to Alençon, she learned the art of producing the fine lace for which the town was famous throughout Europe.

Louis and Zélie were married in 1858 and over the next fifteen years had nine children. Sadly only five lived to adulthood. The deaths of two sons and two daughters occurred within a period of three years and deeply grieved the loving couple, who found solace only in their faith. When the youngest child, Marie-Françoise-Thérèse, was born on the second day of 1873, she was frail and ill. Fearing that tragedy was about to visit them once again, the Martins prepared for yet another shattering loss. But the child who was destined to be a saint somehow survived, and within a year became a happy, healthy baby. Surrounded by love, she grew into a high-spirited, affectionate girl, who indulged in both frequent laughter and occasional tantrums. She delighted her parents and four older sisters.

Thérèse's early years were filled with great but short-lived happiness. Sorrow entered the lives of the Martins in August of 1877, when Zélie succumbed to cancer. Thérèse, only four years old and unable to comprehend what had happened, began to turn inward. The laughing child became a quiet and shy one. Her older sister Pauline tried to act as a substitute mother for Thérèse, but the effect of Zélie's death was profound.

It was then that the family moved from Alençon to Lisieux, the town which has become inextricably linked with the name of Saint Thérèse. Here the Martins once again found hope, consolation, and healing in their faith. It soon became the custom of Louis and Thérèse to visit different churches each day to pray before the Blessed Sacrament.

At the age of eight the little girl went to school, and although not happy there, she did well. Eventually she was promoted to a class in which most of the girls were older than she. Their academic ability, however, was often less than hers. This led to her being resented. It increased her sense of isolation and made her focus on her family. Yet even a stable family life, so basic to the happiness of a child, was denied to Thérèse, because Pauline—the little girl's anchor of stability—was soon to enter the Carmel of Lisieux. Of this difficult moment Thérèse later wrote, "In one instant I understood what life was; until then I had never seen it so sad, but it appeared to me in all its reality and I saw it was nothing but a continual suffering and separation."[2]

In the year after Pauline's entrance into Carmel, Thérèse suffered a long and mysterious illness marked by fever, weakness, and hallucinations. As she lay ill, there grew steadily within her a desire for a life of prayer and contemplation—for the life of Carmel. By the time she regained her health—something which she attributed entirely to our Lady—this desire had become firm. Though she was only ten years old, it was a desire which would never wane.

It seems strange to think of one as young as Thérèse going through a kind of spiritual torment, but she did during this period, suffering an intense longing for God, as well as strong attacks of scruples. Her father, fearing for his daughter's health, decided she should be educated at home by tutors. It was at this time that she became very close to her sister Marie, who, like Pauline before her, became Thérèse's substitute mother. Even here, instability intruded, as Marie, too, felt a strong vocation to the enclosed life and began to make plans to follow Pauline into Carmel. So at the age of thirteen, Thérèse had lost a mother figure—for the third time.

Sadness, isolation, and loss seemed destined to be her lot, and perhaps such things would have been the case in the life of some other child, but Thérèse Martin seemed to have access to a source of strength and resilience not readily available to many. On Christmas Eve of 1886, on the way home from Midnight Mass, something inexplicable happened. Thérèse began to see things differently. Her fears and self-doubts evaporated; her sadness disappeared. For the first time since Zélie's death, she became again the happy, confident child she once was. She also became even more certain of Carmel as her destiny and said that her heart suddenly became so full of charity that she forgot herself and began to think only of others. Her goal now was clear: it was to bring other souls to Christ.

Convinced that Carmel was where she could do the greatest good for Christ, Thérèse requested to be received. She was kindly but quickly turned away because of her age. Undaunted and absolutely determined, Thérèse, her father in tow, went to the bishop to request a special dispensation. Not getting the response she had hoped for, Thérèse resolved to go to the Pope himself. The year 1887 was the golden anniversary of Pope Leo XIII's priestly ordination, and Catholics throughout Europe were going to Rome for the occasion. Thérèse, her father, and her sister Céline went, as well. And in an audience with the pope, Thérèse did the unthinkable. Unbidden, she walked up to the Holy Father, knelt at his feet, and tearfully asked his permission to enter Carmel, despite her age, which was still only fifteen. "Go," said the pope. "You will enter if God wills it."

Apparently God did will it, for on New Year's Day in 1888, one day before Thérèse's sixteenth birthday, the prioress of the Lisieux Carmel granted her permission to enter. Thérèse was elated and soon entered the cloister, never again to emerge. But this joyous moment, too, had its difficulties. Louis Martin's health was now in decline. He had begun a descent into dementia. His death would come in only a few years.

Thérèse spent a mere nine years in Carmel before her death, and she spent those years as a good and faithful nun, who was in no way spectacular. She was certainly not another Saint Teresa of Avila. She seemed to have much goodness but nothing of greatness about her. She wrote poetry and was eventually selected to be mistress of novices, but there is nothing terribly unusual in this. She prayed fervently for priests and conducted long correspondences with two of them, always encouraging and helping whenever possible. This, too, is common. However, although her outward life in Carmel did not seem extraordinary, deep within her soul Thérèse was living a different life, a life of profound spirituality which was centered on what she called her "little way," transforming all the tasks of her day, all the moments of her life into little acts of love, which she continually offered to God. This "little way," so different from the paths of many saints, was her vehicle to sanctity, her road to God.

On the night between Holy Thursday and Good Friday of 1895, Thérèse suffered the first signs of tuberculosis, the illness that would end her earthly life in two years. Earlier, she had offered herself as a sacrificial victim to the merciful love of God. Now this offering took on a special meaning; it would become the focal point of her life. For some months her disease worsened until she suffered what was surely a true crucifixion.

Her deep inner spiritual life had always been hidden, and now the great spiritual trials she faced would also be hidden. These came to light only through her memoir, the book we have come to know and love as *The Story of a Soul.* Pope Benedict XVI quotes Thérèse at this stage: "I am assailed by the worst temptations of atheism. Everything has become questionable, everything is dark."[3] He then says:

> She feels tempted to take only the sheer void for granted. In other words, in what is apparently a flawlessly interlocking world someone here catches a glimpse of the abyss lurking—even for her—under the superb structure of the supporting conventions. In a situation like this, what is in question is not the sort of thing that one perhaps quarrels about otherwise—the dogma of the Assumption, the proper use of confession—all this becomes absolutely secondary. What is at stake is the whole structure; it is a question of all or nothing. That is the only remaining alternative; nowhere does there seem anything to cling to in this sudden fall. All that can be seen is the bottomless depths of the void into which one is also staring.[4]

Thus we find Thérèse to have depths that might seem dangerous to us; we see what we had imagined to be a flawless faith start to crumble. The smiling young nun who offers us roses is suddenly gone to be replaced by one who seems no better than we are. With Christ on the Cross and with all of us she cries out: "My God, my God why have you abandoned me?" It is a shattering moment. But it is only a moment. For Thérèse, like Christ, was not abandoned; the darkness was not the final word. It was to be overcome by the light of grace, supplanted by a renewed and even-more-brilliant faith. Thérèse, who had worked so endlessly to give herself to God, received in the end the grace to find the God who is revealed when everything else is ripped away, when all the comforts of religion and of the world are gone and all hope is obliterated. This saint we love to sentimentalize peered into the abyss of nothingness and triumphed over it, triumphed so completely, that in her last moments she could open her eyes, gaze at the crucifix which had been placed in her hands and murmur, "My God, I love You!"

A Lifelong Journey with a Childhood Friend

About seventy years ago I was a child in second or third grade in Catholic school in New Jersey, and like most children I had a good number of friends. Casual friendships are very common at that time of life; among the very young, friends tend to come and go quickly. I remember some of them; others I can hardly recall. One thing I remember very well, however, is that it was at this point that I made a new friend, a very special one, for that was the time that I ran into "the Little Flower." Saint Thérèse turned out to be a wonderful friend, one who's stuck with me through thick and thin ever since. She's a friend who lets you mature at your own pace; she seems childlike and completely understandable when you're very young, but by the time you've become an adult you begin to realize how profound she really is, how much she has to teach us. As a boy I depended on her, counted on her to understand my problems and even to solve them for me. As an adult I never tire of looking into the great depths of this wonderful and yet wonderfully simple soul. Saint Thérèse was a very popular and attractive saint for Catholics when I was a boy, and she seemed the perfect saint to me then. I've changed my mind about many things since early grade school, but this isn't one of them. There's no Catholic who couldn't benefit by developing a devotion to—making a friend of—Saint Thérèse. In a way Thérèse is always with me. Sometimes she follows me. Usually she leads, and I know I can depend on her as you can only depend on a true friend.

Like all good friends we speak often. There is rarely a day that passes that I do not pray to Saint Thérèse. As a consequence, from the time I was a boy, I wanted very much to see Lisieux, to see the places where Thérèse lived her short life. I was blessed to have the opportunity to go there, to visit the convent in which she lived and to pray to my friend in the magnificent basilica that now stands near the convent. I remember that time often. It is important to me.

Why? Why does this young, devout girl mean so much to me and to so many other people? My own life has been very different from hers, and her experience of the world was quite different from mine. To put it mildly, I think we are extremely different personalities. She seemed born for prayer and contemplation, for the stillness of the cloister. Although I have spent more than half a century in religious life, I have always known (and I'm sure those who know me will agree) that I was never meant to be a contemplative. My goal was always to work with the poor.

No matter what kind of life we lead, no matter how different we are from her, however, Thérèse has something to say to us, even when we are most troubled. In her own life she faced something that we usually try to avoid, something that life often thrusts in our path: that darkness can close in on a person, even one who is very close to God. Many people live at least part of their lives in darkness of one form or another without others really knowing. Sometimes we are afraid to tell others; sometimes we cannot even find the words. Saint Thérèse is our companion in this, for none of those who knew her realized that toward the end of her life this optimistic and simple young nun was really walking in the valley of the shadow of death. Through trust in God, however, she emerged from this darkness, and she can be our guide in emerging, as well.

So, I urge you to let Saint Thérèse become your friend. Join the countless people who have been devoted to her for many years. Read her autobiography and ponder it. Let her childlike simplicity become an antidote to the fast-paced but meaningless lives so many of us lead. Let this great friend teach you to trust God even when things seem darkest. This is a saint who said, "I will spend my heaven doing good on earth." I take her at her word, and I suggest you do, too. I doubt that you'll be disappointed.

———

The following is a letter that Thérèse carried on her heart on the day of her profession as a Carmelite nun. I believe it says much about this simple but great saint.

O Jesus, my Divine Spouse! May I never lose the second robe of my baptism! Take me before I can commit the slightest voluntary fault. May I never seek nor find anything but Yourself alone. May creatures be nothing for me and may I be nothing for them, but may You, Jesus, be *everything!* May the things of earth never be able to trouble my soul, and may nothing disturb my peace. Jesus, I ask You for nothing but peace, and also love, infinite love without any limits other than Yourself; love which is no longer I but You, my Jesus. Jesus, may I die a martyr for You. Give me martyrdom of heart or of body, or rather give me both. Give me the grace to fulfill my Vows in all their perfection, and make me understand what a real spouse of yours should be. Never let me be a burden to the community, let nobody be occupied with me, let me be looked upon as one to be trampled underfoot, forgotten like Your little grain of sand, Jesus. May Your will be done in me perfectly, and may I arrive at the place You have prepared for me.[5]

SAINT TERESA BENEDICTA
OF THE CROSS

AT FIRST GLANCE, the life of Edith Stein, Saint Teresa Benedicta of the Cross, may seem to be a series of contradictions and surprises. To some, it may even appear to end in senseless tragedy. I believe, however, that this saint's life reveals something far different and far deeper than this. In the extraordinary story of Edith Stein we see the providential hand of God guiding a soul slowly but steadily through the twists and turns of life, leading a fragile human being ever closer to Him and to eternal joy, sometimes through moments of terrible suffering. Edith Stein came to prominence at the end of the First World War and was swallowed up in the savagery of the Second. She died when I was just nine years old; thus she is a saint for our time. Let us now take a look at this unusual saint, a Jewish woman who spent her early years as an avowed atheist, a respected philosopher who became a devout Catholic, a Carmelite nun who became a martyr.

A SAINT IN AUSCHWITZ

The eleventh and youngest child of a Jewish family who lived in Breslau, Germany, Edith Stein was born on October 12, 1891—the date of Yom Kippur, the Jewish Day of Atonement, that year.

Despite the fact that her family was religious, Edith was not. Early in her life, she lost not only faith in the Jewish religion but faith in God Himself, and by her thirteenth year she called herself an atheist. Gifted with exceptional intelligence, Edith enrolled in the University of Breslau and later at the University of at Göttingen at a time when very few young women were accepted for study at the university level. Her academic work was focused primarily on philosophy, and she was soon acknowledged as one of the brightest students of her generation.

Although strongly drawn to the academic life, Edith worked as a nurse for the Red Cross during the First World War. There she saw firsthand the carnage that resulted from this first modern war. In 1916 she began studies for her doctorate at the University of Freiburg, where she met Edmund Husserl, a renowned philosopher and originator of the philosophical method known as phenomenology.[1] It was not long before the talented young woman became Husserl's assistant, a position coveted by young intellectuals throughout Germany. One of those was Martin Heidegger, who (despite his later complicity with the Nazis) is considered by many to be among the greatest philosophers of the modern period.

During the summer of 1921, when Edith was nearing her thirtieth birthday, she visited some friends for a few days. Having nothing to do one evening, she searched among their bookshelves for something to read. As if by chance, she came upon the autobiography of Saint Teresa of Avila and soon found herself so immersed in the book that she read throughout the night to finish it. By morning Edith knew that something had happened to her during the reading of this book; a profound shift had occurred. The God whom she had so decisively rejected now seemed somehow real and present to her, and she felt a strong attraction to the Catholic Church. She began taking instruction and was baptized early the following year, but even this was not enough. Soon after her entrance into the Church, this former atheist felt a call to the religious life, a call to the Carmel of Saint Teresa.

Her spiritual director urged her to wait, to give her vocation time to mature, and so Edith wrote, lectured, and taught at several Catholic institutions for a few years. The promising university career that had seemed to be her destiny began to become ever more uncertain during this period. Anti-Semitism and the Nazi party in Germany were growing in power, making it increasingly difficult for Jews and people of Jewish descent to secure university positions.

Finally in 1933, shortly before Hitler's fateful election as Chancellor of Germany, she received permission to enter the Carmel at Cologne-Lindenthal. She did so with joy, taking the name Sister Teresa Benedicta of the Cross—a name that would later seem prophetic.

As the atheist had become a Catholic, so in Carmel the philosopher became a mystic. Edith had studied the great Carmelite mystical writers Saint Teresa of Avila and Saint John of the Cross avidly before she had entered the convent. Now they became her great models as she gave herself more and more to the contemplation of the God she had once so completely denied. Deeply Christ-centered, Edith's constantly growing spirituality focused more and more on the Cross, on Christ's passion and sufferings. Perhaps she could sense that the shadow of the Cross was about to fall over her own life, as well.

The persecution of Germany's Jews escalated during Edith's time in Carmel, becoming overt and violent in 1938, which in November of that year saw the destruction that marked *Kristallnacht*.[2] Fearing that her continued presence at a German Carmel might endanger the other sisters, Sister Teresa Benedicta transferred to a Carmel in Echt, Holland. The effort, however, bought only a little time. On May 10, 1940, Germany invaded Holland and imposed the same anti-Jewish laws they had used at home.

Sister Teresa Benedicta of the Cross managed to live relatively undisturbed for another two years, although she and her sisters were surely aware that any moment might bring disaster. In 1942 the Nazis commenced the deportation of Dutch Jews to concentration camps in the east, an action the Dutch Catholic Bishops quickly and strongly opposed. In retaliation the Nazi overlord, Arthur Seyss-Inquart, ordered the deportation of all Jews who were Christians by conversion or by partial parentage, people who up to this point had been exempt.

It was only a matter of days before Sister Teresa Benedicta of the Cross was arrested. With her was her sister Rosa, who had also converted to Catholicism and was living at the Echt Carmel. The two were eventually sent to Auschwitz, where Sister Teresa Benedicta spent her time caring for those who could not care for themselves. In the words of a Jewish businessman who survived the camp:

> Among the prisoners who arrived on 5 August Sister Benedicta made a striking impression by her great calm and composure. The misery in the camp and the excitement among the newcomers were indescribable. Sister Benedicta walked about among the women, comforting, helping, soothing like an angel. Many mothers were almost demented and had for days not been looking after their children, but had been sitting brooding in listless despair. Sister Benedicta at once took care of the poor little ones, washed and combed them, and saw to it that they got food and attention. As long as she was in the camp she made washing and cleaning one of her principal charitable activities, so that everyone was amazed.[3]

On August 9, 1942, Sister Teresa Benedicta of the Cross ended her earthly life in the gas chambers of Auschwitz. She died there for her Jewishness, yet she was profoundly Christian. In her death, as in her life, she accepted the Cross of Christ with great courage and with great faith in the God to whom she had dedicated herself. In the life of Saint Teresa Benedicta of the Cross we find a truth that we modern people like to ignore, that the Cross of Christ is the center of all things and must be at the center of our lives if we are to be truly Christian.

THE SHADOW OF THE CROSS

Everyone of my generation was deeply affected by the horrors of World War II. When I was a small child in New Jersey the war was at its height, and I spent quite a lot of time trying to imagine what was happening in Europe and in the Pacific, to imagine what the battles were like, what war was like. I remember the looks on the faces of parents as they anxiously awaited news of their sons who were in the Army or Navy. I can only imagine how difficult it was to learn that a loved one had been killed alone and so far away. As did most people, I praying constantly about the war. I prayed for peace and for all the young men who came from my hometown and were now in the service. I prayed for what seemed like forever before peace was finally a reality. Such memories and feelings stay with me, and I am sure they stay with many people of my age. We were too young to play a role in the war but old enough to have some grasp of the enormity and tragedy of it.

After the war we learned more. We learned of heroism and disaster, of unimaginable cruelty and spectacular courage and selflessness. We also learned of martyrs—and there were many of them. Among those whose stories began to make their way to this country and to be told in schools and churches was that of a Carmelite nun whose name I had never heard as a child: Sister Teresa Benedicta of the Cross. As I learned more and more about her I found myself drawn to her almost more than to any of the others. I later learned that other people felt the same way, that for many of my generation Sister Teresa Benedicta of the Cross was *the* martyr of the Nazis.

At least part of this attraction, I am sure, came from the fact that—amazingly—this Carmelite nun was Jewish. As we learned after the war of the unspeakable horrors of the Holocaust and the unimaginable cruelty that became commonplace in the Nazi treatment of the Jews, we were astonished and horrified. Reality seemed to have become worse than our most frightful imaginings.

Perhaps our fascination with Sister Teresa Benedicta of the Cross had something to do with trying to connect ourselves somehow with those people who had been so terribly abused. This Catholic martyr who was born Jewish seemed to provide us with a link, a real connection.

A friend of mine who has studied the writings of all the great Carmelite saints once said to me that there is something dark in the writings of Saint Teresa Benedicta of the Cross. How could it be otherwise, for she confronted the problem of evil in a very real way? She must have seen her end coming; she must have known that her conversion to Catholicism and her status as a member of Carmel would not save her.

The miracle of Saint Teresa Benedicta of the Cross is, I think, that in her turn from atheism to the Church and her eventual entrance into Carmel, she found the grace to withstand the overwhelming evil that was coming like a great wave to engulf her and so many more. In the midst of Auschwitz she did not lose hope; as she watched her people being mercilessly sacrificed on the altar of Nazism, she did not renounce her conversion; when the entire world looked hopeless, she did not relapse into the atheism of her youth.

Even though the world was going up in flames around her, flames she knew would consume her, she was able to maintain the peace of Christ within her. This—in case you need to be told—is the mark of a saint. And so it wasn't too many years after the war that Sister Teresa Benedicta of the Cross became *Saint* Teresa Benedicta of the Cross.

We all face the problem of evil in our lives—not as Sister Teresa Benedicta of the Cross did, but in many smaller ways. We—who are not saints—often become discouraged. We are often plagued by doubts. We demand to know where God is, where Christ is. We ache with disappointment when our most fervent prayers seem to go unanswered—unheard.

It is at these difficult moments that we should turn to Saint Teresa Benedicta of the Cross, for in this gentle Carmelite who died a martyr to both the Jewish people and the Catholic Church, we will find the courage to continue. We will find the faith to believe in the God who seems so silent, so unmindful of us at times. Pray to Edith Stein, to Saint Teresa Benedicta of the Cross, when you face an evil that seems too great for you. Pray for the grace that was given so generously to her that enabled her to overcome what was surely one of the greatest evils the world has ever known.

Saint Teresa Benedicta of the Cross died a terrible death in Auschwitz when I was a boy, living safe and sound in New Jersey. I am a rather old man now, and the Nazis who brought her earthly life to an end are but memories. The horrors of that awful war are beginning to be forgotten by many. They fade into the past, becoming mere history, not reality. Yet the reality that persists is that of a Jewish scholar who found Christ through the writings of Saint Teresa of Avila, of a Carmelite nun who triumphed over the evil that seemed to consume her, of a saint who knew that God was with her, even in Auschwitz.

———

The writings of Saint Teresa Benedicta of the Cross are voluminous. Many of them are densely written philosophical works. Perhaps the most famous of these is On the Problem of Empathy, *which is a phenomenological study of empathy. Here we will not look at her philosophical works but only at a short excerpt from an essay titled "Love of the Cross" and subtitled "Some thoughts for the Feast of Saint John of the Cross." These words were written when Saint Teresa Benedicta was living at the Carmel in Echt, Holland. It shows that she was very aware that the Cross would soon come to her own life. Although brief, this excerpt gives us much food for thought:*

The burden of the cross that Christ assumed is that of corrupted human nature, with all its consequences in sin and suffering to which fallen humanity is subject. The meaning of the way of the cross is to carry this burden out of the world. The restoration of freed humanity to the heart of the heavenly Father, taking on the status of a child, is the free gift of grace, of merciful love. But this may not occur at the expense of divine holiness and justice. The entire sum of human failures from the first Fall up to the Day of Judgment must be blotted out by a corresponding measure of expiation. The way of the cross is this expiation. The triple collapse under the burden of the cross corresponds to the triple fall of humanity: the first sin, the rejection of the Savior by his chosen people, the falling away of those who bear the name of Christian.

The Savior is not alone on the way of the cross. Not only are there adversaries around him who oppress him, but also people who succor him. The archetype of followers of the cross for all time is the Mother of God. Typical of those who submit to the suffering inflicted on them and experience his blessing by bearing it is Simon of Cyrene. Representative of those who love him and yearn to serve the Lord is Veronica. Everyone who, in the course of time, has borne an onerous destiny in remembrance of the suffering Savior or who has freely taken up works of expiation has by doing so canceled some of the mighty load of human sin and has helped the Lord carry his burden. Or rather, Christ the head effects expiation in these members of his Mystical Body who put themselves, body and soul, at his disposal for carrying out his work of salvation. We can assume that the prospect of the faithful who would follow him on his way of the cross strengthened the Savior during his night on the Mount of Olives. And the strength of these cross-bearers helps him after each of his falls. The righteous under the Old Covenant accompany him on the stretch of the way from the first to the second collapse. The disciples, both men and women, who surrounded him during his earthly life, assist him on the second stretch. The lovers of the cross, whom he has awakened and will always continue to awaken anew in the changeable history of the struggling church, these are his allies at the end of time. We, too, are called for that purpose.[4]

18.

SAINT MAXIMILIAN KOLBE

MAXIMILIAN KOLBE IS A FELLOW FRANCISCAN. He is also a model of sanctity, courage, and a trust in God so profound that it seems to leave no aspect of his life untouched. Here we find a saint who came from the humblest of beginnings and did not even live to see his fiftieth birthday; yet Maximilian Kolbe accomplished astonishing things for God, usually against overwhelming odds and often despite illness and persecution. This is a saint whose life should still have great meaning for us seventy years after his execution in Auschwitz, a saint who should inspire us to rise above our limitations and to trust in God as we confront life's difficulties.

Most people know little of this wonderful saint beyond the story of his tragic death. This is a shame, for he lived an amazingly productive life dedicated to God and our Lady. So I am very pleased to be able to tell you something of this great saint.

THE SAINT OF MARY IMMACULATE

Born to devout parents on January 8, 1894, in a small town in present-day Poland,[1] he was given the name Raymond. The future saint's parents were poor. Just to keep their family fed, they worked as basket weavers, farmers, grocers, and mill workers.

Raymond was a pious child, perhaps even a truly spiritual one. His parents were devoted to our Lady and taught their son to be so, as well, and it was this devotion that transformed his life. It almost seems as if he was chosen by God for Mary, a soul selected to be utterly devoted to the Blessed Mother. (It is hard to imagine a more perfect realization of Saint Louis de Montfort's concept of "consecration to Jesus through Mary" than Maximilian Kolbe.) As a boy of twelve he experienced what he described as a dream (but what some have called a vision) of the Blessed Mother. His description of it is moving, even haunting:

> I asked the Mother of God what was to become of me. Then she came to me holding two crowns, one white, the other red. She asked me if I was willing to accept either of these crowns. The white one meant that I should persevere in purity, and the red that I should become a martyr. I said that I would accept them both.[2]

I do not think it excessive to say that the meaning of this dream guided him for the rest of his life; and, as we shall see, these startling words were to be prophetic.

Only a year after this dream, in 1907, an utterly determined thirteen-year-old Raymond Kolbe and his elder brother Francis decided they could wait no longer before dedicating their lives to God. They illegally crossed the border between Russia and Austria-Hungary and made their way to the Conventual Franciscan[3] junior seminary in Lwów. Raymond studied there, so excelling in mathematics and physics that a brilliant career in science was predicted for him. But nothing could dissuade him from his goal, and in 1910, at the age of sixteen, he was finally allowed to enter the novitiate. He professed his first vows one year later, adopting the name Maximilian. Three years after that, he professed his final vows in Rome, where he had been sent to study for the priesthood. At this moment he changed his name to Maximilian Maria, to emphasize his great devotion to the Blessed Mother.

Almost every stage of Maximilian Kolbe's life seemed marked by urgency, by a strong need to accomplish what he believed God wanted him to do. Perhaps he understood in some way that earthly time for him was to be short, that he was not destined to live to an old age. Yet the thought of illness and death seemed to leave him undaunted. In his mid-twenties he was diagnosed with a serious case of tuberculosis. This would have stopped most people in their tracks, but it only made Maximilian Kolbe redouble his efforts. By the time he was ordained in 1918, he had already been instrumental in founding the Crusade of Mary Immaculate, with the aim of "converting sinners, heretics, and schismatics, particularly freemasons, and bringing all men to love Mary Immaculate."[4]

After World War I he returned to Poland, which was now an independent country. Firmly believing that the rebirth of his beloved nation was due to our Lady's intercession, Father Maximilian labored tirelessly to introduce the Crusade of Mary Immaculate to Poland. Soon it was established throughout the country. His tuberculosis worsened, but he worked harder and harder. By the beginning of 1922 he was publishing a monthly periodical, the *Knight of the Immaculate*, in Krakow. He started producing five thousand copies at a time—a number many people thought was far too many. They were wrong; within five years Father Maximilian was printing seventy thousand copies, and even this was not enough. The *Knight of the Immaculate* became so popular that larger quarters had to be obtained in order to print it, and some land donated by a nobleman became Father Maximilian's new home. He called this land the City of Mary Immaculate. Consisting of little more than a few shacks at first, the City of Mary Immaculate soon became a large friary complete with a junior seminary. By the late thirties, it was entirely self-supporting and had a population of nearly eight hundred people. The *Knight of the Immaculate* was now printing an amazing 750,000 copies each month. Other publications were begun, as well as a radio station, and it has been said by many that there was a tremendous upsurge in devotion in Poland during this period as a direct result of Father Maximilian's work.[5]

As if this were not enough, in 1930 Father Kolbe turned his gaze to mission lands and with four friars made his way to Japan. There he founded a Japanese version of the *Knight of Mary Immaculate* as well as an outpost of the City of Mary Immaculate.[6] Far Eastern countries are notoriously impervious to Christian missionaries, but Father Kolbe's efforts met with success. He founded a novitiate and a junior seminary. Soon the Japanese edition of the *Knight of Mary Immaculate* was publishing sixty-five thousand copies each month.

Some people feared for Father Kolbe when he left Europe for Japan. They suspected that he would be strongly opposed and perhaps even killed. Instead he earned the respect and admiration of the Japanese and established good relations with both Buddhist and Shinto[7] priests. In 1936, fearing for Father Maximilian's deteriorating health, his superiors recalled him to Europe and—they thought—safety. They had no idea that they were really calling him to his death.

World War II began in 1939, and Poland was quickly occupied by the Nazis. After being briefly deported to Germany that year, Father Maximilian was allowed to return (on the Feast of the Immaculate Conception!) to his beloved City of Mary in Poland. Although weak and ill he immediately set to work to protect all he could from the carnage of war. Under his direction, three thousand Polish refugees, of whom about two thousand were Jews, were sheltered in the City of Mary Immaculate. He and his friars shared everything they had, often going without food themselves to feed others.

The Nazis permitted him to publish one edition of the *Knight of Mary Immaculate* in early 1941. This was something they soon regretted because Father Maximilian did exactly what he always did: spoke God's truth without fear. He wrote:

> No one in the world can change Truth. What we can
> do and should do is to seek truth and to serve it when we

have found it. The real conflict is the inner conflict. Beyond armies of occupation and the hecatombs of extermination camps, there are two irreconcilable enemies in the depth of every soul: good and evil, sin and love. And what use are the victories on the battlefield if we ourselves are defeated in our innermost personal selves?[8]

Father Maximilian was arrested soon after that fateful issue of the *Knight of Mary Immaculate* was published and was sent to Pawiak, a notorious prison near Warsaw. There, despite his illness, as a priest he was singled out for special torment. On one occasion an SS guard asked him if he believed in Christ. Father Maximilian replied that he did, and the guard struck him. Then the guard asked the same question. Receiving the same answer, he stuck the priest again. This went on and on, the guard beating Father Maximilian over and over again and Father Maximilian relentlessly proclaiming his faith in Christ despite the beating.

It wasn't long before Father Maximilian was transferred to Auschwitz. There he faced forced backbreaking labor every day. Still, he carried on his priestly life as best he could, hearing confessions, praying with terrified prisoners, and even celebrating Mass with bread and wine that had been smuggled in.

In July 1941 there was an escape from Auschwitz. In retaliation and in order to deter other escape attempts, the deputy camp commander selected ten prisoners for execution. Francis Gajowniczek, a married man with young children, was among them. Filled with compassion for the young man, Father Kolbe stepped forward and offered to take his place. The Nazis were astonished and demanded to know why he would do such a thing. Father Kolbe responded, "Because I am a Catholic priest," and with those simple words he grasped the red crown of martyrdom offered so many years before by our Lady.

The ten men were brought to a single large cell and left there to starve. Father Maximilian encouraged the others with songs, prayers, psalms, and meditations on the Passion of Christ. After two anguishing weeks, six of the men had died, and three more were unconscious. Only Father Maximilian, despite his frailty, was still conscious. Unwilling to wait any longer the Nazis killed these four with injections of poison on August 14, 1941.

The life of Maximilian Kolbe shows the power of God shining through human weakness. It demonstrates the miracles that faith and compassion can accomplish. In Saint Maximilian Kolbe we find a clear demonstration that the human will and the human spirit, when united to the will of God, are holy and truly unconquerable.

A LIGHT IN DEEPEST DARKNESS

The life of Saint Maximilian Kolbe has stirred the hearts of countless Catholics, other Christians, and Jews in the latter part of the twentieth century. Out of the horror of the Second World War and the carnage caused by the Nazis there emerged a number of accounts of people of extraordinary courage and faith. All of these stories are inspiring. However, the story of Maximilian Kolbe seems to me to be, if not unique, then very unusual. When we think of the Second World War, we often think in terms of huge numbers of people, of the millions killed and displaced, of whole populations exterminated. Yet it was not to save millions or thousands or even hundreds of people that Maximilian Kolbe sacrificed his life. It was to save one man, one soul infinitely loved by God.

In Maximilian Kolbe's heroic death we find an act of love that seems so extravagantly wasteful that it can only be Christian. If he had done nothing he might have survived. He might have lived to reestablish his work after the war, and he might have helped many people. Yet he chose not to consider any of that, not to weigh the possibilities of his future against one endangered life. He chose instead to die for a man he did not even know.

I believe he chose to die for one life in the same way that Christ would have died to redeem just one sinner. In Maximilian Kolbe's heroic act, we find a powerful affirmation of the value of human life, of the sacrificial love that each Christian is called to have for others at every moment. This saint was well aware that each human life is of infinite worth in God's eyes, and he acted on this knowledge.

I once had the opportunity to meet Francis Gajowniczek, the man for whom Maximilian Kolbe sacrificed his life. As you might expect, his life has been greatly affected by what happened to him. He has never forgotten and has done an extraordinary amount to make people aware of the holiness and heroism of the Franciscan priest who died for him. I heard him speak in Polish, telling of his experience with Saint Maximilian. I realized, as I watched him and listened to his words, which were translated into English for us, that Gajowniczek was a very ordinary man who had simply been caught up in the tidal wave of world history. He was not a martyr or a hero; he was simply a man who loved his family and wanted desperately to return to them. Yet the life of this ordinary man has been made extraordinary by one great act of selfless love. He was also an immensely grateful man despite the tragic fact that, although he survived, his family was killed before he could return to them.

I remember that it seemed somehow awesome to listen to this man, fascinating, yet troubling. In fact, I actually had lunch with him that day. Let me tell you, I was very uncomfortable eating a meal and thinking of Saint Maximilian being starved to death. It was the most uncomfortable lunch I ever had.

I felt the same way when I visited the cell in which he was starved to death. A visit to Auschwitz—a place of so much horror, yet also a place in which great heroism and faith existed—is always deeply moving, but standing in the cell in which Saint Maximilian ended his earthy life was a very powerful experience for me. On a visit to Auschwitz in 1980 Pope John Paul II left a

Paschal candle burning in the middle of that cell, a symbol of the triumph of Christ over sin and death in a place of incredible sin and death. It was Christ's light burning brightly and dispelling the awful darkness of that place. Saint Maximilian was like that candle. The light of his life banished the darkness for at least one soul, and that is no small accomplishment.

I have been to other places that were important in the life of Saint Maximilian, including *Mugenzai no Sono*, his friary in Nagasaki. Because if its position, which is on the side of the mountain that faces away from the city, it escaped major damage when the atomic bomb was dropped on the city. Only a few windows broke, so this place is much the same as when he left it during the 1930s. Again I felt in awe of this great Franciscan saint, this great "knight of Mary Immaculate" who lived so intense and complete a Catholic life.

Saint Maximilian Kolbe is an inspiration to us all, but he should be a special inspiration to priests. Most priests are good men who struggle along in life pretty much in the same way other people do. Priests have the same confusions and mediocrities as everyone, and sometimes the life of a priest can become as mundane as anyone else's. We can become prone to doing things out of habit just as anyone else can. In the life and death of Maximilian Kolbe, however, we have a great image of a priest who lived out his priesthood to the maximum degree, a priest who trusted in God and in our Lady completely and who accomplished great things through them, a priest who made the greatest of sacrifices for a stranger. How could he not be a constant inspiration to us all?

———

The following is a brief excerpt from Saint Maximilian's writings concerning consecration to Jesus through Mary. It is beautiful and shows the great intensity of his devotion to our Lady.

To draw close to Her, to make ourselves like Her, to allow Her to take possession of our heart and of all our being, that She might live and work in us and through us, that She Herself love God with our heart, that we belong to Her without any reserve: behold our ideal.

To shine in our environment, to conquer souls for Her, in such wise that in Her presence the hearts of our neighbors also open, so that She might extend Her reign in the hearts of all who live in any corner of the earth, without regard to difference of race, of nationality, of language, and likewise in the hearts of all who will live in any moment of history, until the end of the world: behold, our ideal.

Further, that Her life be ever more deeply rooted in us, from day to day, hour to hour, moment to moment, and this without any limitation: behold our ideal.

And still, that this Her life develop in the same way in every soul which exists or will exist in any time: behold our precious ideal.[9]

SAINT PIO OF PIETRELCINA

WE WILL CONCLUDE our little book on saints with a look at one of the most fascinating characters that God has given the Church in a long, long time: Saint Pio of Pietrelcina. Known the world over as Padre Pio, this humble Capuchin-Franciscan—who never left his native Italy—has captured the imaginations of countless people the world over. We have already dealt with two of his contemporaries, Edith Stein and Maximilian Kolbe. Although all three were born within a few years of each other and each entered religious life in Europe, only Padre Pio survived the Second Word War. He died in 1968, which—as some of my older readers are quite aware—is really not very long ago at all.

Padre Pio may seem to be something of a mystery, or perhaps it might be better to call him an enigma. He may even be troubling to some because his life appears to contradict so much of what the modern world has taught us to believe. In a way Padre Pio seems a medieval saint who was born out of season. He lived during a time when skepticism and secularism were growing by leaps and bounds. Throughout much of Padre Pio's life people like the Protestant New Testament scholar Rudolf Bultmann and his many fashionable disciples were proclaiming that no modern person could possibly believe in the miracles of the New Testament.

Yet similar miracles regularly attended the life of Padre Pio, and these have been affirmed by many.

Like Saint Francis and Saint Catherine of Siena, Padre Pio was a stigmatist. He mysteriously bore the wounds of Christ, and in his case the stigmata lasted for half a century. His wounds were often studied by physicians, none of whom could explain them or offer a reason why they never became infected; neither could they produce a theory as to how a man could lose blood constantly for decades without suffering any noticeable ill effects. Padre Pio also had the gift of healing and even of bilocation at a time when these were thought mythological—even laughable. He was able to discern spirits during an era that proclaimed spirits to have reality only in our unconscious minds. And these were only a few of the miraculous spiritual gifts given by God to this holy Capuchin. So let's take a look at the life of Saint Pio of Pietrelcina, one of the most fascinating saints of our time, and see what he has to teach us.

THE SAINT WHO BORE THE WOUNDS OF CHRIST

Fittingly named for Saint Francis of Assisi, Francesco Forgione was born on May 25, 1887, to Giuseppa and Grazio Forgione in the southern Italian village of Pietrelcina. The Forgione family, which also included one other son and three daughters, was very devout. Although in our time a high level of religiosity in an entire family might be considered something of a rarity—even an oddity—this was nothing unusual in Pietrelcina, a town noted for its fervent Catholicism. One might even go so far as to say that in Pietrelcina the Church was as much a part of people's lives as the air they breathed. It was certainly a setting in which a religious vocation could be nourished and encouraged.

The Forgione family, like most people they knew, were sturdy peasant farmers. Although they had little education and, in fact, were barely literate, they were so well versed in Scripture that they had memorized large sections of it to recite to their children.

They were also very conversant with the Church's practices and tradition, if not her theology. Little Francesco grew up immersed in faith, prayer, and devotion. Daily Mass, the Rosary, and regular fasting were natural and vital parts of life in the Forgione family, and from his early childhood Francesco seemed to possess a depth of piety rare in one so young. He felt drawn to the priesthood almost from the moment he was old enough to articulate the desire, and at about the age of ten he encountered a young Capuchin friar. This brief meeting seemed to put Francesco on the road for which he was destined. From that point on he was determined to be a Capuchin.

Proud of their son, Francesco's parents took him to the closest Capuchin monastery to speak of his vocation. While the friars saw real promise in the boy, he was far too young to enter and his education consisted of only three years of basic schooling. This was something that had to be remedied before the order could consider him.

While we might think it strange for parents to take so seriously a child's desire for a religious vocation, people looked at things differently at the time. In fact, the Forgione family undoubtedly viewed the possibility of their son's entering the Capuchins as a great gift from God. They were so determined that Francesco should become a friar that Grazio, the boy's father, made the dramatic move of going to America to work for a couple of years in order to procure enough money to hire a tutor for his son. This he did, and the boy's academic deficiencies were overcome.

On January 6, 1903, the Solemnity of the Epiphany, Francesco Forgione, now all of fifteen, entered the Capuchin novitiate. When it came time for him to take his first vows, he chose the name Pio (Pius in English) in honor of Saint Pius V, the patron saint of his hometown. Brother Pio made his final vows in 1907 and was ordained to the priesthood on September 7, 1910.

Up to this point the life of Francesco Forgione (now Padre Pio) did not appear to be very different from the lives of many devout young men who entered the priesthood or religious orders. But this was appearance alone and was soon about to change. The deep inner life of this young priest was about to become manifest, showing him to be so different from those around him as to be literally unique. Within about a month of his ordination Padre Pio was deep in prayer when he is said to have experienced an apparition of both Jesus and Mary. At that time he also received the stigmata for the first time. His doctors were astounded and confused, and Padre Pio prayed that the wounds would be taken from him, but not because he didn't want to suffer in the way Christ suffered. His problem in his own words was: "I do want to suffer, even to die of suffering, but all in secret." In other words, he did not want the attention that the stigmata was sure to bring him. His prayers were answered, and the wounds simply disappeared, but the amazing events of Padre Pio's life were just beginning.

About a year later one of the brothers found Padre Pio in a state that seemed the brink of death. Thinking it was too late for any help, the brother ran to the chapel to pray for his dying confrere. When he returned, Padre Pio was absolutely normal, as if nothing unusual had happened. He had been in ecstasy—between heaven and earth. This was only the first of many remarkable ecstasies that were to become part of Padre Pio's life.

Plagued with ill health, Padre Pio spent about five years back in Pietrelcina, still living the life of a friar but with his family. He returned to community life in 1916 and was sent to San Giovanni Rotundo, a place with which he was destined to be closely connected for much of his life. As World War I drew to a close, he gave spiritual direction and taught seminary students. After the outbreak of the war, the friars, one by one, had been drafted into military service. Finally Padre Pio was, as well. Assigned to the Medical Corps, he became unhappy, almost despondent, and his health—which was always precarious—began to fail. In a fairly short time Padre Pio found himself in the hospital, where he spent most of the rest of the war. He was discharged in March 1918, thankful to return to San Giovanni Rotundo.

On July 27, in response to Pope Benedict XV's plea for prayers for the end of the war, Padre Pio offered himself to God as a victim for the end of conflict. A few days later he had a vision of the wounded Christ, who pierced Padre Pio's side just as His own side had been pierced by the Roman soldier's lance. This wound was not just spiritual or psychological: a physical gash actually appeared in the priest's side. Only a few weeks later, Padre Pio was at prayer and the same vision reappeared. This time the encounter with the wounded Christ left Padre Pio marked with a gift for which he became known throughout the world: the stigmata. It was never to disappear again during his earthly life. From that moment he was to bear the wounds of Christ constantly and publicly for five long decades.

Shortly after the end of the First World War, word that Padre Pio had received the stigmata began to spread. The war had been an absolutely shattering experience for Europe. Virtually an entire generation of young men had lost their lives; nations that had existed for centuries had been dismantled and new nations formed out of them. It was clear that nothing would be the same again. The immense destruction of World War I and the uncertainty that resulted from it seemed to contradict the very idea of a loving God, and many people throughout Europe found their faith shaken to its very foundations. Many despaired, turning to an agnosticism that often bordered on nihilism. At this difficult moment, Padre Pio suddenly seemed like a beacon of light in a sea of darkness. Here was someone whose very existence proclaimed the presence of God. Here was a man who demonstrated by bearing the wounds of Christ that God is not indifferent to our trials and agonies but suffers with us as we endure them. People began to see this Capuchin priest as a sign of hope; they also began to make their way to San Giovanni Rotundo. Soon the town was nearly overrun by pilgrims, many of whom had come great distances and (since there were no hotels) often had to sleep outside the monastery.

Padre Pio welcomed them all. He often worked for up to nineteen hours each day, meeting with pilgrims, hearing their confessions, and celebrating Mass for them. Often the demands on his time became so great that he would sleep for only two hours each night, but this never seemed to daunt or even affect him.

It was during the sacrament of reconciliation that Padre Pio's uniqueness was most apparent. He often heard confessions for up to twelve hours a day, and he continued this grueling schedule even when he was elderly and in failing health. He was regularly able to read the hearts and souls of the people who came to him for confession, reminding them of sins they had forgotten, seeing deeply into thoughts they were too ashamed to put into words, or finding exactly the right way to help them deal with persistent failings. In this manner Padre Pio brought countless people to God.

Although he was only doing the work that God wanted him to do, a man as dramatically different from others as was Padre Pio can hardly avoid antagonizing skeptics, and so he developed his share of detractors. Numerous people accused him of various infractions over nearly half a century. These ranged from complaints that Padre Pio's celebration of the Mass took too long (he was known for lengthy and very pious celebrations of the Eucharistic liturgy) to venomous attacks accusing him of immorality of various kinds. All of these were shown to have no basis in fact. Despite the lack of truth in these allegations the Vatican did place various restrictions on Padre Pio at times. All were eventually lifted, and no wrongdoing was every found.

In 1940 Padre Pio convinced three doctors to come to San Giovanni Rotundo to help in the creation of a new hospital, which he called the Home to Relieve Suffering. It took sixteen long years before the doors of this facility were finally opened and in the course of those years Padre Pio was once again accused of wrongdoing, this time regarding inappropriate use of funds. Again the charges were proved ridiculous, and the hospital only enhanced his reputation. From this point onward even larger numbers of pilgrims came to him, and they came from the farthest reaches of the world.

He lived only a little more than ten years more, exactly as he always had. His life was given to prayer, the Eucharist, and hearing confessions. He never tired of helping the people who came to him day after day, and during all this time the stigmata he bore continued to astonish the world. Some still maintain that the blood that dripped from his wounds smelled of perfume. In his last days Padre Pio was in very poor health. It was all he could do to say Mass. Yet he persisted almost up to the day of his death, which was September 23, 1968. On that day, exhausted and ill, Padre Pio made his last confession and went home to God after so many years of doing God's work on earth. The stigmata, which he had born for over half a century, disappeared and for the first time in anyone's memory Padre Pio's body was at last whole.

How Padre Pio Once Came to My Rescue

When I was in high school the Catholic world was filled with much discussion of Padre Pio. Almost everyone was fascinated by this humble Capuchin who seemed so closely connected to God that the miraculous had become the commonplace in his life. But this was not the only reason he attracted our attention. The intensity, the tangibility, of the holiness of this man not only affected other souls; it even seemed to affect governments. To this day many people—including some who speak with real authority—believe that it was Padre Pio who kept his native Italy from becoming Communist during the difficult postwar period. Once, when Padre Pio was still alive, I heard the Father General of the Capuchin Order say that it was Padre Pio who had prevented the Italian communists from coming to power because "the ordinary people listened to him." If this is so, then the world owes an enormous debt to Padre Pio. Imagine what would have happened in Europe during the forties, fifties, and sixties if a large and populous communist state had existed at its very center.

The simplicity of Padre Pio and the miraculous nature of his stigmata stumped the experts, and I can remember as a high-school boy being very pleased that this was so. Controversy abounded around this Capuchin, and there were even theologians in the Church who were skeptical. I always noticed, though, that the skeptics were those who had never met him, those who had never bothered to make the trip to San Giovanni Rotundo.

Of course none of this bothered Padre Pio. In fact, he couldn't have cared less. He simply went about his daily task of offering his solemn Mass and hearing hours and hours of confessions every day. I have spoken to people whose confessions he heard, and they always said that he was able to reveal things about themselves they had not told him—sometimes things they had worked for decades to keep hidden. There was once a disbelieving woman who wanted to trip up Padre Pio in the confessional. When she was done reciting her supposed sins there was slight pause, and then Padre Pio said to her: "Aren't there a few things that you forgot?" He then told her not only her sins but her purposes for being there in the confessional. She told this to me later, and she told many other people, as well, and I have no doubt that it is a true story.

When I was a novice and a young Capuchin there was no living soul who seemed more worthy of imitation than Padre Pio. I was absolutely convinced that he was a living saint, but he was very far away. I hoped one day to go to Italy and meet him and wondered what it would be like if he heard my confession. I wanted to be present when he celebrated Mass. Well, I never did meet him face-to-face, but once when I needed help he came to me in a way that I will never forget.

After about nine years in the religious life, I was told that I was about to undergo a big change. Somehow I had been chosen to begin higher studies in Rome and was about to be sent there to become a New Testament scholar. I was rather surprised to learn this, but I did all that I was told to do to prepare, including trying to master Koine Greek, the language in which the New Testament was written. Only a few weeks before I was to be ordained a priest I was busy translating some Greek passages when the rector of the seminary appeared at my door. He told me in a rather abrupt and even cold way that I needn't continue with my language study. I was not to be sent to Rome after all. I was confused, speechless, and very hurt.

As it turned out, this change had been the result of something I had said—or rather something I had asked. William F. Buckley, the conservative writer, had come to speak to us, and I, along with another young brother, had questioned some of his ideas and conclusions. This was done in a very respectful way, but it had been enough to scuttle my future as a Scripture scholar.* In those days I was seen as something of a dangerous liberal, a word whose meaning is completely different today. So there I sat in my room, my Greek text open before me—and my future suddenly a blank.

The rector disappeared, but in only about three minutes he was back again. I braced myself for more disappointment but it didn't come. Instead he handed me an envelope and said, "This is a letter that has just come to you from Europe." The return address was San Giovanni Rotundo.

With shaking hands I opened it to find a note from a layman, a friend of mine who had visited San Giovanni Rotundo. He had asked Padre Pio to write something to a young friar who was about to be ordained. The envelope also contained a very typical old-fashioned holy card, which showed a priest's hands holding a chalice. On the back, in an old man's handwriting was written in Italian: "Jesus alone will be your strength and your comfort." It was signed "Padre Pio, Capuchin." I must say that if the Archangel Michael had walked into my room at that moment I could not have been more impressed. I went on for the next few weeks

---

* God moves in mysterious ways.

to my ordination smiling and with a sense of joy that would not have been there if not for that card and those few words. My lack of a future as a Scripture scholar now seemed a very bearable cross. Those who knew that I had just been shot down wondered what was going on. They couldn't believe that I was not crushed. I had been crushed, but Padre Pio had changed all that. I believe he had been sent to me at a very painful moment in my life.

He is still my friend, and although we never met I speak to him regularly. I have always treasured those few words he wrote to me. They were the most perfect words possible and it gives me great strength and joy to remind myself of them every day of my life.

———

The following are excerpts from letters written by Padre Pio. They clearly show both the intensity of his personality and his overwhelming love for both God and man.

The thought of being unable to bring spiritual relief to those whom Jesus sends me, the thought of so many souls who foolishly want to justify their evil in defiance of the Chief Good afflicts me, tortures me, martyrs me, overcharges my mind and rends my heart . . . Of late I have felt two desires growing gigantically within my spirit . . . I want to live, so as to be of use to my brethren in exile, and on the other hand, I wish to die to be united with my heavenly Spouse.[1]

Everything can be summed up in this: I am devoured by the love of God and the love of my neighbor. God is always fixed in my mind and stamped in my heart. I never lose sight of Him. I can admire His beauty, His smiles, His vexation, His mercy, His vengeance or, rather, the rigors of His justice.[2]

I feel nothing except to have and to will that which God desires. And in Him I always feel at peace, at least within my soul. Externally, sometimes I am somewhat vexed for the sake of my brothers.[3]

AFTERWORD

AND SO THERE IT IS, a bit of my personal litany of the saints. I could have continued writing many more chapters because there are many more saints who mean a great deal to me, many more saints whom I consider to be my friends. Perhaps someday I will write about them if God gives me the time and the ability. But I think I've said enough for the moment, and I hope that this book has started you thinking about saints and the importance they should have in your life.

We live in a world that is marked by loneliness. The American philosopher Thoreau said that most people lead lives of "quiet desperation," and the truth of this statement is born out all around us every day. Families are separated by divorce and remarriage or by great distances. Elderly people are shunted aside in nursing homes and quietly forgotten. People live in tiny apartments in buildings that contain hundreds of such apartments. Often those people have never spoken to their next-door neighbor. We "text" to each other rather than speak to each other. The list goes on and on. Relationships are made difficult by a thousand things in our society. The sense of isolation only grows with each passing year.

But a Catholic is never really alone because we are never isolated from the saints. This great "cloud of witnesses" is with us from our earliest moments, and it remains with us through eternity. It has been my goal in this book to show that the saints truly are *with* us. They are the friends who will never desert us, the ones who always want what is truly best for us. The most isolated person on the face of the earth is really not isolated at all—in fact, he is rich in companionship—if he has a relationship with the saints.

In churches we often see stained-glass windows of saints with sunlight steaming through them. I consider that to be a symbol of a great reality. The life of a saint is a life through which God's glory shines; it streams like light through those stained-glass windows. As we become more and more familiar with the saints we see the different ways that God's love and power are revealed, for each saint is unique, and we see God acting in the life of that saint in a unique way.

I offer you here in the closing pages of this book a great adventure—the adventure of life with the saints. No matter who you are or what your experience is, there is a saint—and probably many saints—who will speak to you. Find those saints through study and prayer, and form relationships with them. Turn to the great "cloud of witnesses" that God has so lovingly provided for us. I guarantee your life will never be quite the same.

I can find no more fitting way to close this little book than with the opening prayer for the Solemnity of All Saints. I hope that it will be truly an "opening prayer" for many, a prayer that marks the opening of many lives to the saints:

God our Father,
source of all holiness,
the work of your hands is manifest in your saints,
the beauty of your truth is reflected in their faith.
May we who aspire to have part in their joy
be filled with the Spirit that blessed their lives,
so that having shared their faith on earth
we may also know their peace in your kingdom.
Grant this through Christ our Lord. Amen.[1]

NOTES

Chapter 1. Saint Ignatius of Antioch

1. The first seven councils of the Church are: First Council of Nicaea (325), First Council of Constantinople (381), Council of Ephesus (431), Council of Chalcedon (451), Second Council of Constantinople (553), Third Council of Constantinople (680), and Second Council of Nicaea (787).

2. From the Epistle of Ignatius to the Magnesians.

3. Simon Critchley, *The Book of Dead Philosophers* (New York: Vintage Books, 2008), 249.

4. *The Liturgy of the Hours* © 1974, International Committee on English in the Liturgy, Inc. (All rights reserved) as found in *The Office of Readings* (Boston: The Daughters of Saint Paul, 1983), 770-771.

Chapter 2. Saint Augustine

1. We must remember that in the Church's early centuries infant baptism was rare.

2. At about the same time as the birth of Augustine's son, his father, Patricius, died after finally converting to Christianity.

3. Saint Ambrose, who was then Bishop of Milan, was one of the Church Fathers and the first Doctor of the Church.

4. Before he had journeyed very far, however, he encountered the Cross of Christ, facing the death of his beloved mother and his only son, the two people who meant the most to him.

5. Karl Barth, *Epistle to the Romans* (New York: Oxford University Press, 1968), 85-86.

6. William Barrett, *Irrational Man* (Garden City: Anchor Books, 1962), 96.

7. *The Liturgy of the Hours* © 1974, International Committee on English in the Liturgy, Inc. (All rights reserved) as found in *The Office of Readings*, 81-82.

Chapter 3. Saint Monica

1. The indigenous peoples of North Africa west of the Nile Valley.

2. It should be stressed that Monica's faith was very orthodox. It was simply a few minor cultural accretions to her religious practice to which Saint Ambrose objected.

3. Saint Augustine, *Confessions*, trans. Henry Chadwick, (Oxford: Oxford University Press, 1991), 172.

4. *Confessions*, 170-171.

Chapter 4. Saint Benedict

1. Despite this experience, Benedict did not favor the life of a hermit for most people, believing instead that very few are called to this unusual vocation. He also thought that the life of a hermit should be attempted only after one has already lived successfully in religious community.

2. The rule of a religious order or community is really a compilation of rules. It describes in detail the way the members are to conduct their lives.

3. One of Benedict's great contributions is what he called the *Opus Dei* or the Divine Office (Liturgy of the Hours). This is the great sequence of prayers, psalms, and readings, which the monk places at the center of his prayer life. Each day the monk is called to the Divine Office seven (formerly eight) times. Thus prayer is never far in the future or in the past. The Divine Office forms a rhythm of prayer that suffuses the monk's (or nun's) life.

4. *The Holy Rule of Saint Benedict,* trans. Rev. Boniface Verheyen (Grand Rapids, Michigan: Christian Classics Ethereal Library), 2.

Chapter 5. Saint Francis of Assisi

1. Boniface Hanley, OFM, and Salvador Fink, OFM, *The Franciscans, Love at Work* (Paterson, New Jersey: St. Anthony Guild Press, 1962), 15.

2. *The Franciscans, Love at Work,* 18.

3. Ten years after this meeting the Franciscans numbered 3,000.

4. For more on Saint Clare, see the next chapter.

5. As Christ instructs in Mark 6:7.

6. *Francis and Clare: The Complete Works*, trans. Regis Armstrong, OFM Cap., and Ignatius Brady, OFM, Classics of Western Spirituality (New York: Paulist Press, 1982), 151.

Chapter 6. Saint Clare

1. *The Franciscans, Love at Work*, 198-9.
2. Ibid., 199.
3. Ibid., 213.
4. *Francis and Clare: The Complete Works*, 192.

Chapter 7. Saint Catherine of Genoa

1. Some of Catherine's fasts were nearly unbelievable, such as eating absolutely nothing during the entire season of Lent. She, however, thought them quite ordinary.
2. Catherine did not join him in this.
3. *Catherine of Genoa: Purgation and Purgatory, The Spiritual Dialogue*, trans. Serge Hughes, Classics of Western Spirituality (New York: Paulist Press, 1979), 72.
4. Should this ever come to pass she will be the first married laywoman so honored.
5. *Catherine of Genoa: Purgation and Purgatory, The Spiritual Dialogue*, 71-72.

Chapter 8. Saint Thomas More

1. Carthusian monastery.
2. Thomas More, *De Tristitia Christi*, in *The Complete Works of St. Thomas More*, vol. 14, ed. and trans. Clarence H. Miller (New Haven, Connecticut: Yale University Press, 1976), 413.

Chapter 9. Saint Teresa of Avila

1. Her illness was most likely a form of malaria.
2. Soliloquy #10 in *The Collected Works of St. Teresa of Avila*, Volume One, trans. Kieran Kavanaugh, OCD, and Otilio Rodriguez, OCD (Washington, DC: ICS Publications, 1976), 382-383.
3. Teresa of Avila, *Way of Perfection*, trans. E. Allison Peers (New York: Image Books, 1991), 198.

Chapter 10. Saint John of the Cross

1. *An Anthology of Spanish Poetry from Garcilaso to Garcia Lorca*, ed. Angel Flores (Garden City, New York: Doubleday and Company, Inc., 1961), 63.

2. Even today the Carmelite nuns and friars of the reform are known as "discalced" or shoeless.

3. *The Spiritual Canticle*, found in *The Collected Works of Saint John of the Cross*, trans. Kieran Kavanaugh, OCD, and Otilio Rodriguez, OCD (Washington DC: ICS Publications, 1979), 551.

Chapter 11. Saint Peter Canisius

1. The ecumenical council called by Pope Paul III in 1545 to deal with the effects of the Protestant Reformation. It lasted until 1563.

2. Quoted from an unpublished manuscript in the Father Hardon Archives.

3. Ibid.

4. From Pope Benedict XVI's General Audience given on February 9, 2011.

Chapter 12. Saint Martin de Porres

1. *The Liturgy of the Hours* © 1974, International Committee on English in the Liturgy, Inc. (All rights reserved) as found in *The Office of Readings*, 1618-1619.

Chapter 13. Saint Benedict Joseph Labré

1. Quoted from memory by Father Benedict J. Groeschel, CFR.

Chapter 14. Saint Catherine Labouré

1. We have seen that Saint Teresa of Avila did the same thing upon the death of her mother. I believe that this was a natural reaction for both of these bereaved young girls but wonder if it would be a natural reaction today when our understanding of God and our sense of what it means to be a saint in eternal life is so sadly diminished.

2. Sr. Juana Elizondo, *A Light Shining on the Earth* (Bowling Green, Missouri: Editions du Signe, 1997), 11.

3. Ibid., 11.

4. Ibid., 12.

5. We must not forget that this occurred twenty-four years before the doctrine of Mary's Immaculate Conception was approved.

6. Quoted in Joseph I. Dirvin, CM, *Saint Catherine Labouré of the Miraculous Medal* (New York: Ferrar, Straus & Cudahy, Inc., 1958), 229-230.

Chapter 15. Saint Bernadette Soubirous

1. François and Louise Soubirous actually had nine children of whom Bernadette was the eldest, but four died in infancy.

2. *A Holy Life: The Writings of Saint Bernadette of Lourdes*, ed. Patricia A. McEachern, PhD (San Francisco: Ignatius Press, 2005), 20.

3. Ibid.

4. The doctrine of the Immaculate Conception had been promulgated only four years before.

5. *A Holy Life: The Writings of Saint Bernadette of Lourdes*, 23

Chapter 16. Saint Thérèse of Lisieux

1. Joseph Cardinal Ratzinger, *Introduction to Christianity* (San Francisco: Ignatius Press, 1990), 17.

2. *The Autobiography of St. Thérèse of Lisieux*, trans. John Clarke, OCD (Washington, DC: ICS Publications), 58.

3. Quoted in *Introduction to Christianity*, 18.

4. *Introduction to Christianity*, 18.

5. *The Autobiography of St. Thérèse of Lisieux*, 275

Chapter 17. Saint Teresa Benedicta of the Cross

1. Phenomenology has been found very useful by many religious figures, including Pope John Paul II, whose 1953 doctoral dissertation dealt with the work of Max Scheler, one of Edmund Husserl's disciples and one of Edith Stein's teachers.

2. Sometimes called "the Night of Broken Glass," this was a Nazi-provoked series of attacks on Jews throughout Germany, which occurred on November 9, 1938.

3. Quoted in Hilda C. Graef, *The Scholar and the Cross* (Westminster, Maryland: Newman Press, 1955), 128.

4. *The Collected Works of St. Edith Stein, Volume II*, ed. L. Gerber and Michael Linssen, OCD (Washington, DC: ICS Publications, 1992), 245.

Chapter 18. Saint Maximilian Kolbe

1. At that time Poland had not been an independent country in over a century. Its territory was completely divided among Russia, Germany and Austria-Hungary. Although the area in which the Kolbe

family lived was totally controlled by the Russian Tsar, the desire for freedom still burned brightly among its residents.

2. Mary Craig, *Blessed Maximilian Kolbe, OFM Conv.: Priest Hero of a Death Camp* (London: Catholic Truth Society, 1973), 2.

3. Franciscanism had been part of Raymond's life from the beginning, as both his mother and father were committed Franciscan tertiaries.

4. Mary Craig, *Blessed Maximilian Kolbe, OFM Conv.: Priest Hero of a Death Camp* (London: Catholic Truth Society, 1973), 5.

5. Maximilian Kolbe brought so many people to a life of renewed faith that after World War II the Polish bishops sent an official letter to the Vatican claiming that it was Father Kolbe's work that had prepared the Polish people to endure and survive the horrors of the war.

6. It is hard not to notice that this saint, who perished in the horrors of the Second World War, chose Nagasaki, of all places, to establish his work in Japan. It was one of the two cities that would be destroyed by nuclear bombs during that war. Despite the overwhelming destruction in Nagasaki, however, *Mugenzai no Sono* (the Garden of Mary Immaculate), which is what Father Kolbe called his friary, survived. It was saved by its location on a steep hill that slanted away from the blast. Today it's the center of a Conventual Franciscan province.

7. The native religion of Japan.

8. Mary Craig, *Blessed Maximilian Kolbe, OFM Conv.: Priest Hero of a Death Camp* (London: Catholic Truth Society, 1973), 8.

9. In *The Kolbe Reader* (Libertyville, Illinois: Marytown Press, 1987).

Chapter 19. Saint Pio of Pietrelcina

1. Cited in C. Bernard Ruffin, *Padre Pio: The True Story* (Huntington, Indiana: Our Sunday Visitor, Inc., 1982), 166.

2. Ibid.

3. Ibid.

Afterword

1. *The Roman Missal* © 1973, International Committee on English in the Liturgy, Inc. (All rights reserved) as found in *The New Saint Joseph Sunday Missal and Hymnal* (New York: The Catholic Book Publishing Co., 1986), 1414.